SPENSER'S UNDERWORLD
IN THE 1590 *FAERIE QUEENE*

SPENSER'S UNDERWORLD
IN THE 1590 *FAERIE QUEENE*

Matthew Fike

Studies in Renaissance Literature
Volume 24

The Edwin Mellen Press
Lewiston•Queenston•Lampeter

Library of Congress Cataloging-in-Publication Data

Fike, Matthew.
  Spenser's underworld in the 1590 Faerie queene / Matthew Fike.
    p. cm. -- (Studies in Renaissance literature ; v. 24)
  ISBN 0-7734-6670-3 (hc.)
    1. Spenser, Edmund, 1552?-1599. Faerie queene. 2. Epic poetry, English--History and criticism. 3. Voyages to the otherworld in literature. 4. Knights and knighthood in literature. 5. Future life in literature. 6. Death in literature. 7. Hell in literature. I. Title. II. Series.

  PR2358.F54 2003
  821'.3--dc21

                                                                    2003046349

This is volume 24 in the continuing series
Studies in Renaissance Literature
Volume 24 ISBN 0-7734-6670-3
SRL Series ISBN 0-88946-143-0

A CIP catalog record for this book is available from the British Library

          The Edwin Mellen Press   The Edwin Mellen Press
                 Box 450   Box 67
          Lewiston, New York   Queenston, Ontario
          USA 14092-0450   CANADA L0S 1L0

                 The Edwin Mellen Press, Ltd.
                 Lampeter, Ceredigion, Wales
                 UNITED KINGDOM SA48 8LT

          Printed in the United States of America

For my father

TABLE OF CONTENTS

PREFACE

Scholarly interest in Edmund Spenser has been growing for the last few decades with an encyclopedia published in 1990, an annual entitled *Spenser Studies*, a *Spenser Newsletter* which has recently become *The Spenser Review*, published three times a year, and a new variorum of all the works in progress. The most reread and reanalyzed of those works is, of course, *The Faerie Queene*, one of the most provocative and longest poems in the English language. The study of the present book, *Spenser's Underworld*, is certain to raise issues for a rethinking of much that has been published about the poem and its characters and for further significant research and examination. Matthew Fike has taken on a subject that has had attention paid to it, for Hell appears as both a physical place and a state of damnation, a significant place in Spenser's moralized landscape, as Thomas E. Maresca tells us in the entry on Hell in the encyclopedia. But in his chapters, which deal with only the first three books of the epic, Fike evinces a greater presence for the Harrowing of Hell in the poem, a different understanding of what Sir Guyon, the hero of temperance in Book II, exhibits in his encounter with the enchantress Acrasia in her Bower of Bliss, and a view of Merlin in relation to Britomart in Book III than have been standard readings. The pervasiveness of the *ars moriendi* tradition in the Renaissance enters tellingly and strategically, leading to revaluations of the underworld that lies at the base of so much action in the poem. Fike recognizes, as well, that the *ars vivendi* tradition is thus provoked as counter to reap reward in one's descent into the nether world of death. Perhaps to be remarked is the "Puritan" belief in the Harrowing of Hell by Christ which became a dominant theme of dissension in the end of the sixteenth and the beginning of the seventeenth centuries. Spenser's reading of the days between the Crucifixion and the Resurrection places him firmly against the Catholic and Anglo-Catholic beliefs of the time.

Books I-III of the poem were first published in 1590, with indication that the total poem was to be in twelve books or possibly even twenty-four. In 1596 three more books were added (with an alteration at the end of Book III to effect a smooth joining of the two parts), and in 1609 (after Spenser's death) two cantos of an alleged seventh book and two additional stanzas usually assigned to an eighth book were printed. The 1590 publication has been classified as a finished unit examining private virtue, the 1596 additional books thus setting forth public virtue. Fike adds to that differentiation the motif of the Harrowing of Hell and its classical epic adaptation in the descent to the underworld of Odysseus and of Aeneas as a unifying factor in that first set of books. While it has been seen to function in the poem beyond its single reference in I.x.40, the specific readings involving Sir Guyon and Britomart have not been previously offered. Guyon, the argument goes, is not exhibiting temperance in the Bower of Bliss, he is exemplifying continence, for he has been confronted with temptation and he resists even though tempted. The reexamination causes Fike to discuss the widespread prostitution of the Elizabethan period, establishing a linkage with the action surrounding Acrasia's enticement for Guyon. Neither continence (nor incontinence) nor prostitution is a subject treated in the encyclopedia.

But perhaps it is Britomart's presentation that will disturb more people, for she is a *female* hero and thus a celebrated example for our modern age. As the champion of chastity (with double meanings involved), she has not emerged as one who, in the Malecasta episode and the House of Busirane or in her dealings with Merlin, has engaged anything akin to the Harrowing of Hell. Yet she does receive a wound from Gardante, suggesting some succumbing to the weakness that ogling (the meaning of Gardante's name) implies. She does descend to Merlin's cave where she becomes more assured and comes to act in strong contrast with Merlin's infernal parody of Christ. She will go on to rescue Amoret from Busirane's enchantment. The biblical and the epical descents into the underworld become clear, so presented.

Fike works through foreshadowing in the poem, through the contrasts between characters and events, through numerous parallels in the poem and in classical literature such as the *Aeneid*. Corroborating his readings of these matters are the writings of Sigmund Freud and Carl Jung appropriately enough, for the epic has long been recognized as a spatial and psychological construct. The allegoric interfacings of characters and events equating qualities of person, fictive but actual people, historical (or supposedly historical) figures, can be read in terms of Freudian concepts of superego, ego, and id, and of Jungian archetypes. This book will raise resistance from some, but the new readings that this examination of the import of the underground particularly in religious belief in Spenser's masterpiece cannot be ignored.

John T. Shawcross

University of Kentucky

ACKNOWLEDGEMENTS

I am grateful to several journals that published earlier versions of the following: Chapter Two ("'Not without Theseus': The Mythic Weave of *The Faerie Queene*, Book 1," *Classical and Modern Literature* 17.3 [1997]: 231-49), Chapter Three ("Prince Arthur and Christ's Descent into Hell: *The Faerie Queene*, I.viii and II.viii," *ANQ* 12.2 [1999]: 6-14), Chapter Five ("Spenser's Merlin Reconsidered," *Spenser Studies* 13 [1999]: 89-99), and Chapter Six ("Britimart and the Descent into Hell," *ANQ* 10.4 [1999]: 13-18). This material appears here with the permission of Heldref Publications, *Classical and Modern Literature*, and *Spenser Studies*.

I received assistance and support from numerous persons and institutions as I worked on *Spenser's Underworld*. John Knott guided my initial exploration of *The Faerie Queene* while I was a graduate student at the University of Michigan. Charles Huttar taught me the craft of professional literary scholarship, helped me upgrade all stages of this book, and along with Russell Meyer reviewed the penultimate draft for The Edwin Mellen Press. John Shawcross contributed the Preface and provided important support for my work in the 1990s. Peter Schakel shared valuable information and suggestions regarding the publication process. Thomas P. Roche, Jr.'s NEH Summer Seminar, "Virgil, Ariosto, Tasso, Spenser," spurred my thinking in various constructive directions. And librarians Tom Burnett, Judy Avery, and Bob Gorman assisted with reference questions. The Department of English Language & Literature at the University of Michigan provided Visiting Scholar status on several occasions. Finally, the American University in Bulgaria and Winthrop University provided support for conference presentations that contributed to this study.

Numerous family members and friends added their guidance and support.

I am particularly grateful to Francis and Janice Fike, Deborah and Paul Brower, Sue Cronkite, Jeff Lambert, John and Jo Kleis, Hal Kosiba, Gregg Frasco, Bobby Phillips, Peter Bauland, Audrey Fessler, Bill Londo, Sandy Feinstein, David Bucholtz, and Romy Cawood.

INTRODUCTION

Edmund Spenser himself draws attention to the parallelism between the journey of the Redcrosse knight and that of Sir Guyon by calling the latter a "like race to runne" (II.i.32). As in A. C. Hamilton's classic article on the "like race" theme, a standard approach is to view the Legends of Holiness and Temperance as a complementary dyad. A. S. P. Woodhouse holds that Book I is to grace as Book II is to nature, and Thomas E. Maresca treats Books I and II as a unit corresponding to "descent," followed by "illumination" in III-IV, and "ascent" in V-VI.[1] Books I-III of *The Faerie Queene*, however, were published together in 1590, and it is worth considering how all three operate as a unit independent of Books IV-VI, which were added in 1596. The theory that I-III are to private virtue as IV-VI are to public virtue supports to some extent the unity of the poem's early books, but more can be said.[2] The premise of this book is that the underworld provides a further organizing principle in the 1590 poem. Using a range of interpretive strategies to reevaluate episodes that portray or relate to hell, *Spenser's Underworld* argues that Redcrosse, Guyon, and Britomart are on parallel journeys that support a heightened sense of Books I-III as a thematic unit. The book contributes new readings based on analogies to the *ars moriendi* tradition, the Theseus myth, and prostitution; and augments what has been previously published about Arthur, Britomart, and Merlin.

Not surprisingly, the underworld in Spenser participates in the eclecticism of the poem as a whole. To begin with, the poet alludes to two elements of the Christian tradition, Christ's descent into hell and the *ars moriendi*. The relevant background on the former includes the Church Fathers' treatment of Christ's descent into and return from hell, the harrowing of hell in the Gospel of

Nicodemus and Old English poetry, the 16th-century debate on the article of the Apostles' Creed, "He descended into hell," Dante's *Inferno*, and Passus 18 in *Piers the Ploughman*—many of which are addressed in Chapter Three.[3]

The descent-grace-return motif in numerous episodes throughout Books I-III derives from both the tradition of Christ's harrowing of hell and the epic tradition, particularly *Aeneid* VI. The words of Virgil are significant here:

> . . . easy—
> the way that leads into Avernus: day
> and night the door of darkest Dis is open.
> But to recall your steps, to rise again
> into the upper air: that is the labor;
> that is the task. A few, whom Jupiter
> has loved in kindness or whom blazing worth
> has raised to heaven as gods' sons, returned. (VI.175-82)[4]

Later on, Palinurus makes a similar assertion to Aeneas: "I cannot think that you are not prepared / to cross such mighty rivers and the marsh / of Styx without the gods' protection" (484-86). Later still, Charon grumbles, "Indeed, I was not glad to have Alcides / or Theseus or Pirithous cross the lake, / although the three of them were sons of gods / and undefeated in their wars" (517-20). While the two kinds of supernatural enabling mentioned in these passages (direct favor and divine birth) are echoed at various points in *The Faerie Queene*, Spenser Christianizes the motif so that "heauenly grace" (I.v.31), as I demonstrate in Chapter One, assists knights at moments of extreme trial—when they are imprisoned or tempted in dark places underground or assailed by myriad demonic forces. As the Old Testament righteous are liberated from hell (or from the Limbo of the Fathers) not through any merit of their own but through the grace of Christ, so Spenser's knights need or display "actual grace," which is granted for the accomplishment of specific actions or extrication from a difficult situation.[5] Although a thorough analysis of grace in the descent is not my central objective, this study is concerned with Spenser's theology, both in Chapter One on the *ars moriendi* and in Chapter Three on parallel passages related to Calvin's idea of common grace (natural endowment, particularly reason) and Guyon as *microchristus*, a topic on which I align closely with Patrick Cullen's *The Infernal Triad*.[6]

The descent-into-hell motif suggests a primarily literal underground, but there is also a psychological dimension to the underworld, in which the *ars moriendi* tradition participates. The inscription above the entrance to the Inferno ("Abandon hope, all ye who enter here") encapsulates the point. If hell can be a state of despair leading to damnation in a local underworld, then the *ars moriendi* tradition, in which dying persons suffer despair and other demon-related psychological temptations on their deathbeds, is an element of Christian tradition providing an important analogy for the 1590 version of *The Faerie Queene*.[7] Christ's descent may enter into this as well, inasmuch as the *moriens* is said to see the crucified Christ whose despair is one of the possible interpretations of "He descended into hell" in the sixteenth century. Calvin, for example, states that Christ felt "the weight of divine vengeance" and "bore in his soul the tortures of condemned and ruined man."[8] Hell in the 1590 *Faerie Queene* nicely illustrates the fact that hell in the Renaissance, as C. A. Patrides points out, is both a physical place (Hades) and a psychological state (despair).[9] For Spenser there is a clear causal connection between the two: despair, lust, and anger (the principal opponents of holiness, temperance, and chastity) lead to confrontations in places underground or otherwise associated with hell, where a knight either stumbles or is confirmed in virtue.

The local hells in the poem thus have multiple functions. The kind through which Dante travels—a place of torment, damnation, and imprisonment—is clearly one of the types that Spenser creates. The hell to which Duessa descends, the dungeon of Orgoglio, and the torture chamber in the House of Busirane recall the torment of the classical and Christian hells. Located right next to an underworld modeled on *Aeneid* VI, Mammon's cave is a place of temptation, and Arachne's presence in Mammon's cave (II.vii.28) is an ideal metaphor for the entrapment he plans for Guyon. Whereas one needs either actual grace or natural virtue to return from underworlds involving imprisonment or temptation, Merlin's cave—a beneficent place—offers illumination. The magician remarkably uses demonic power to further the divine will without serving the devil or relying on grace. Merlin is poised between the demonic and the divine, and his prophecy's resemblance to that of Anchises in the *Aeneid*, along with other details, suggests the limits of his power and foreshadows his eventual impotence. But his creations—the magic mirror and Arthur's arms and armor—are more permanent. One of Spenser's ironies, then, is that the shield, the poem's clearest symbol of divine grace in Book I, is created by Merlin, the son of an incubus, who wields demonic power for positive purposes.

Although Spenser appropriates many details from Virgil's Hades, he significantly varies the nature and placement of the descent. In Virgil, descent takes place in a single central episode. As a result of Anchises's prophecy, Aeneas's aimlessness, which precedes his descent, yields to zeal for a goal. In other words, his descent brings about a major transformation: in subsequent books he is ever conscious of his goal and of his responsibility. Spenser does use the descent as a major turning point in Book II, Canto 7, where Guyon's journey though Mammon's cave marks his transition from classical to Christian temperance, but more than one episode in Book II recalls the underworld (the Bower of Bliss, as I argue in Chapter Four, alludes directly to the Virgilian underworld). In the middle of Books I and III, however, the respective knights make no pivotal descent, genealogy is part of Britomart's visit to Merlin's cave but otherwise is not included in any kind of descent, and a knight undergoes more than one experience modeled on descents in both classical and Christian traditions. Redcrosse, for example, battles Errour, visits the House of Pride, is imprisoned in Orgoglio's dungeon and kills the dragon. As explained in Chapters One and Two, these episodes echo classical or Christian elements of the descent (sometimes both), and the descent is literal or psychological (sometimes both).

Again, hell in the sixteenth century was considered both spatial and psychological/spiritual. Thus, as Patrides notes, hell pain is both of the senses and of damnation.[10] One does not have to journey underground or suffer physical torture to descend into hell, for hell is also a negative state of the mind's own making. Britomart's visits to Merlin's cave and to the House of Busirane suggest exactly this mixture of spatial and psychological qualities, as do other episodes to be discussed in this book.

There have been many previous analyses of the classical set pieces in Book I, Canto 5, and Book II, Canto 7—Duessa's descent into hell with the wounded Sans Joy and Guyon's journey through Mammon's cave, the latter echoing not only Aeneas's descent but also Christ's three-day harrowing of hell. I will single out two of the most prominent examples to illustrate previous thought and my divergence from it.

Judith H. Anderson's "Redcrosse and the Descent into Hell" provides an excellent explication of the Hippolytus story, which is at the heart of Duessa's descent with Sans Joy.[11] Anderson's association of descent with dreaming works particularly well in the early cantos where Archimago afflicts Redcrosse with various illusions, including a false dream. Her thesis seems particularly attractive in light of Aeneas's descent (the article makes the sleep-death analogy but does not point out that Aeneas's descent may be a false dream because he exits Hades through the ivory gate). Anderson admits that Redcrosse "is not quite so literally asleep at Lucifera's" and that his "visionary experiences begin with a *waking* dream in canto v" (my emphasis).[12] She notes, for example, that Redcrosse is put to bed in stanza 17 but that Spenser never says that he falls asleep. The dream metaphor breaks down even further when Duessa finally returns to the castle in stanza 45 to discover that Redcrosse has already departed. Although dreaming nicely represents the increasing illusion into which he descends, the metaphor is out of sync with the literal sense of interpretation. Duessa's descent into hell certainly does encapsulate various truths about Redcrosse's problems, but it cannot *be* his dream because he could not depart if he were asleep.

Among the finest studies of the classical descent in Book II is Frank Kermode's "The Cave of Mammon," an episode that will be mentioned in Chapter Six primarily for comparative purposes in order to establish the nature of the descent. Kermode asserts that "Guyon undergoes, like Aeneas in the allegorized *Aeneid*, a purgatorial experience, and emerges no longer a knight of mere temperance but an exemplar of heroic virtue and direct instrument of providence. . . . The state into which he passes is that of heroic virtue; he is no longer a temperate man but an active instrument of God."[13] My own reading of Guyon in Chapter Three is that he awakens from the faint not energized with zeal for future achievement (like Aeneas) but aware of fallen man's potential for failure (like Adam). The faint conduces to humility and a realization that grace is necessary: his desires being out of harmony with his reason, Guyon is not a temperate man, much less an instrument of God that transcends temperance.

The last strands of Spenser's treatment of the underworld that are dealt with in this study are native British myth, and Renaissance history: Spenser places Merlin, his most ambiguous magical figure, in a cave, and part of the early modern criminal underworld, namely the realm of prostitution, functions as a relevant analogy for Guyon's encounters with temptresses on his journey toward temperance. The elements of Spenser's underworld, then, are a multi-stranded braid: the Christian faith, classical myth, Renaissance social history, native British myth, and magical diabolism are intertwined rather than discrete, and hell in *The Faerie Queene* is a matter of literal places and negative psychological states.

The present book's organization mirrors that of the 1590 *Faerie Queene*. Chapter One departs from the standard emphasis on rhetorical and pictorial elements to use the *ars moriendi* tradition as a way to explore the demonology of Book I: specifically, to augment a long-standing incomplete gloss of the word "ill" (I.v.31) in relation to diabolism and to reveal the theological complexity of damnation and salvation in the Despaire and House of Holiness episodes.

Chapter Two shows how the Theseus myth parallels and undercuts the Redcrosse knight's adventures in settings that resemble the underworld—the caves of Errour and Despaire, and the House of Pride. The chapter also strengthens the parallelism that others before me note between labyrinth, underworld, and cave; between Ariadne and Una; and between the Minotaur and Errour; and demonstrates that Spenser's treatment of Theseus is consistent with his more general mythic method. Thus the first two chapters strengthen the thematic unity of Book I.

Chapter Three, the first of two chapters on the descent into hell, argues for a position between those of A. S. P. Woodhouse and Patrick Cullen, on the one hand, and Harold L. Weatherby, on the other, by suggesting a continuum of grace rather than the traditional notion that Book I is to grace as Book II is to nature. Contrary to Weatherby, the chapter also asserts that there can be an *imitatio Christi* pertaining only to Christ's humanity.

Stephen Greenblatt's New Historical reading of the Bower of Bliss in *Renaissance Self-Fashioning* proposes three analogies for its destruction: "the European response to the native cultures of the New World, the English colonial struggle in Ireland, and the Reformation attack on images."[14] Chapter Four identifies a fourth analogy—the realm of prostitution—and argues that the knight's continence overshadows his temperance. Specifically, Thomas Coryate's visit to a Venetian courtesan in 1608 and elements of the world of prostitution in Renaissance London (often likened by male participants to a journey into the underworld) are analogies for Guyon's encounters with Phaedria and Acrasia.

Chapter Five challenges William Blackburn's positive view of Merlin's diabolism. Although appearing positive when contrasted with fellow poet-figures Archimago and Busirane, Merlin becomes ambiguous when juxtaposed with Ate, who is first mentioned in the Mammon's cave episode. Merlin is not a lasting challenge to the discord that she represents, a completely effective promoter of marital unity and harmony, or an unqualified figure of goodness. Ultimately, Merlin's ambiguous nature is underscored by Britomart, who combines his beneficence with Ate's ability to act in the world.

Finally, Chapter Six, the second chapter on the descent into hell, challenges Thomas E. Maresca's Neoplatonic theory of descent, proposes an alternate theory, and looks at Britomart's visits to places within the earth (Merlin's cave) and of confinement (the torture chamber in the House of Busirane) as parallels to the experience of Redcrosse and Guyon in terms of the classical-Christian descent and the psychological development it heralds. Being a "like race," her journey in Book III confirms the descent into hell as a unifying principle in the 1590 poem.

CHAPTER ONE

THE ART OF DYING WELL
AND THE AVOIDANCE OF HELL IN BOOK I

Between the late fifteenth and the early eighteenth centuries numerous treatises on the *ars moriendi* were published in England.[1] Often, in these, demons tempt the dying with despair and other inappropriate emotions; the tradition is thus concerned with everlasting damnation in hell. It is surprising that the connection between the tradition and Book I of *The Faerie Queene* has received little attention from critics, since Spenser is assumed to be the translator of Plato's *Axiochus*.[2] In this work, like the angels, saints, and good counselors in the *ars moriendi* tradition, Socrates visits the title character on his deathbed and argues that the soul is immortal and that a blessed afterlife awaits persons who have lived well. The possibility that Spenser translated the dialogue suggests that his interest in the art of dying well predates the 1590 *Faerie Queene* by some ten years. Be that as it may, the standard approach to Spenser's use of the rhetorical and pictorial elements of the tradition is quite valid,[3] but more can be said to illuminate Spenser's use of the tradition in the Despaire episode and in other parts of Book I as well, for the *ars moriendi* is a topos that enables rereadings of numerous episodes. By using the art of dying well to augment a long-standing incomplete gloss and to untangle the theology of the Despaire and House of Holiness episodes, this chapter heightens the sense of the thematic unity within Book I.

A brief summary of the tradition will set the stage for our reevaluation of Spenser's use of the *ars moriendi*. The dying person, or *moriens*, is the central figure in a psychomachia between spiritual forces struggling for his soul. Demons assail him with five temptations, most of which have parallels in Book I: unbelief (Sans Foy), despair (Despaire), impatience, pride/vainglory (the House of Pride/worldly pride, Orgoglio/spiritual pride), and avarice/cupiditas (attachment not only to goods but also to others—e.g., the Redcrosse knight's lustful attachment to Duessa). Meanwhile, angels try to counteract these demonic effects by reminding the *moriens* that Christ's sacrifice has saved far greater sinners.[4]

This contest for the soul of the *moriens* centers on his sins in life. Demons tempt him to despair because of evil deeds he committed earlier in life, while angels and good counselors cite scripture and the Fathers to remind him of God's mercy and forgiveness despite his evil deeds. Tradition has it that the *moriens* also sees the crucified Christ on the cross—even that all dying persons see this image[5]—with two possible results. By conveying the knowledge that Christ died for the *moriens'* sins, the image along with that of the saints may "renewe the infirme mynde of the sycke," but it can also foster a sense of unworthiness and heightened despair.[6] The latter is much like Cassian's *Collationes* in which "knowledge of God brings to the convert a sharper sense of sin—and thus greater grief—than before."[7]

The hour of death was not only written about but also illustrated. Of the eleven illustrations in *The Ars Moriendi* (ca. 1450) two are especially relevant to Book I, Canto 9: "The devil's temptation to despair" and "The angel's good inspiration against despair." The first is filled with devils and human figures that remind the dying man of his sins. The second shows despair successfully resisted: an angel and four pardoned sinners from the New Testament—the thief on the cross, Saul, Peter, and Mary Magdalene—remind the *moriens* that his own salvation is nothing to worry about.[8]

1. "To make ill men aghast": Glossing and the *Ars Moriendi*

Terminal sickness can be interpreted allegorically as the *moriens'* sin, but the *ars moriendi* tradition includes a surprisingly modern sense of causal relationship between sin and sickness, for which writers found support in Lamentations 3:39: "Wherefore then is the liuing man sorowful? man suffreth for his sinne." Caxton claims that "bodyly sekeness cometh of sekenes off soule"; "thynfyrmyte & sekenes of the body taketh his bigynnyng of the langour of the soule." Erasmus states that the *moriens'* friends must "persuade the sycke man . . . that by these meanes [confession, houselynge, and anneylynge] there is more hope to recouer helthe, eyther bycause that a sycke mynd doubleth the soore, or bycause that not seldome the sycknes of the body cometh of the minde, or finally bycause that God sooner wyl here the requestes and prayers for hym that is reconciled than for an vnreconciled person." Likewise, for William Perkins "sicknes comes ordinarily and vsually of sinne. . . . Where the divine ends, there the physition must begin, and it is a very preposterous course that the diuine should there begin where the phisition makes an end, for till helpe be had for the soule, and sinne which is the roote of sicknesse be cured, physick for the body is nothing."[9] In other words, the clergy should not pick up where the doctor leaves off when all is lost; on the contrary, the *moriens'* best hope is that spiritual healing will lead to a physical cure. The latter notion is remarkably close to the idea becoming popular in our own age—that the mind has great potential to affect the health of the physical body, for good or ill. The *ars moriendi* tradition not only equates sin and sickness but also shows sickness arising from a sinful life, not as punishment but as a natural consequence of wrong living.

While the soul affects the body, it is equally true that the state of the body catalyzes the deathbed psychomachia by making the soul vulnerable to demon affliction, and herein lies the most fundamental similarity between the *moriens* and Redcrosse. This point is quite similar to "the close relationship between bodies and souls" that Michael Schoenfeldt sees at work in the Castle of Alma.[10] Whereas he investigates digestion and related processes, the *ars moriendi* literature centers on a person's last moments when eating has ceased and bodily processes are shutting down. Nonetheless, a thread that unifies Schoenfeldt's

treatment of Book II and my investigation of Book I is the effect that "infirmitie /
Of the fraile flesh" has on the soul (II.xi.1). In the case of Redcrosse, the problem
is not improper digestion but extreme deprivation: the knight "is in a state of
unguarded weakness from his sojourn in the dungeon. Arrogance, after all, is the
most weakening opposite of humility."[11] In other words, his intention to attack
the "man of hell" Despaire is arrogant, for the knight's intention is to defeat a
spiritual foe with strength of arms (I.ix.28). For Spenser and for the Renaissance
more generally, there is also in the *ars moriendi* tradition a causal relationship
between sickness and affliction by demons, a sense not limited to Canto 9. The
poet carefully builds into Book I, as a prelude to the Despaire episode, the idea
that sickness of body, mind, and spirit makes one vulnerable to demonic forces.

Spenser makes a key statement about this relationship after Redcrosse
defeats Sans Joy when Duessa and Night are taking the pagan knight to the
underworld for healing.

> Thence turning backe in silence soft they stole,
> And brought the heauie corse with easie pace
> To yawning gulfe of deepe *Auernus* hole.
> By that same hole an entrance darke and bace
> With smoake and sulphure hiding all the place,
> Descends to hell: there creature neuer past
> That backe returned without heauenly grace;
> But dreadfull *Furies*, which their chaines have brast,
> And damned sprights sent forth to make ill men aghast. (I.v.31)

The stanza contains three important points regarding the underworld in *The
Faerie Queene*, all of which bear some relation to the *ars moriendi* tradition and
the situation of Redcrosse.

First, echoing *Aeneid* VI, Spenser points out that it is easy to descend into
hell but hard to return. Assistance is necessary. In classical literature such
assistance comes largely from divine parentage, which is how Hercules and
Aeneas can return. It is also easy to descend into hell in *The Faerie Queene*, but it
is now *divine grace* that helps one return, the kind that Spenser has in mind when
he refers to Christ as "he that harrowd hell with heauie stowre, / The faultie soules

from thence brought to his heauenly bowre" (I.x.40). The *Variorum* records John Upton's comment that Canto 5, stanza 31, alludes "to those creatures that have back returned by Heavenly Grace, being redeemed by Christ, who descended into hell and preached unto the spirits in prison (1 Peter 3.19)."[12] Although the statement specifically refers only to the Old Testament righteous, Dante's successful return with the aid of heavenly grace also lies in the background of Spenser's allusion.[13] Since hell in the poem is both a physical place and a psychological state, divine grace (embodied by Prince Arthur) assists Redcrosse's return from Orgoglio's hellish dungeon and (through Una's reminder of God's mercy) from the despair he feels regarding his misdeeds. As a counter to despair, Una closely resembles the angels and saints in the *ars moriendi* tradition who inspire the *moriens* to hope for salvation.

Spenser's second point in stanza 31 is that "dreadfull *Furies*" and "damned sprights" are the only exceptions to the rule that heavenly grace is required to escape from hell. Furies are clearly infernal in origin, but "sprights" may be either demons, such as those that fetch a false dream for Archimago and others that build Merlin's brazen wall in Book III, or the kind of "damned ghost" or lost human soul mentioned in Canto 9, stanza 49 and Canto 12, stanza 6, which "doen often creepe / Backe to the world, bad liuers to torment" (II.xii.6). Spright means both "disembodied spirit, a ghost" and "a supernatural being, goblin, fairy, etc.," and Spenser uses the word in both senses.[14] Furies when they have broken free of their bonds and lost souls when "sent forth" by God or by Satan can journey from hell to afflict "ill men."

But what are "ill men"? Some editors do not gloss "ill";[15] those who do gloss it assert a single interpretation. Smith and de Selincourt in another context note that "ill-faste" (II.xii.36) means "evil-faced, ugly." P. C. Bayley's 1966 edition of Book I glosses "ill" as "evil, wicked," setting the stage for the present day's editorial consensus. Hugh Maclean's Norton Critical Edition of *Edmund Spenser's Poetry* (1968) glosses "ill" only as "evil." A. C. Hamilton's scholarly

1977 edition of the poem gives only "wicked" as an equivalency.[16] Spenser's consistent use of ill in such negative senses as "unfavorable," "bad," "evil," and "wrongdoing" favors these editors' interpretation of the word and certainly finds support in the *OED*, which notes that "evil" and "ill" have been synonymous since the 12th century. [17] If "ill" means "Evil, in the widest sense . . . ; the opposite of good," then by saying that "damned sprights" make "ill men aghast," Spenser means simply that being a bad person makes one a target for demons or evil human spirits. If "sent forth" from God, they attempt to frighten and correct the evil man; if from Satan, they seek to terrify, punish, and lead the wicked person to despair and damnation.

Alongside various synonyms for "evil," however, *ill* has another meaning in the *OED*: "Of health or bodily condition: Unsound, disordered. Hence of persons (formerly also of parts of the body): Out of health, sick, indisposed, not well." This sense is noted as early as 1460. The *OED* notes the following examples from Spenser's time. Gabriel Harvey says, "I . . . am yet as il almost as ever I was. . . . But as soon as I shall recover mi helth [etc.]." And Shakespeare's Beatrice says in *Much Ado About Nothing*, "By my troth, I am exceeding ill, hey ho" (III.iv.49). In the late sixteenth century, then, "ill" is not just the opposite of "good" but also the opposite of "healthy."

Of course, the notion that poor health leads to supernatural affliction is not exclusive to the *ars moriendi* literature; *Hamlet*, for example, suggests a link between sickness of body/mind/soul and demon affliction. He wonders whether the ghost is "a spirit of health or goblin damned" (I.iv.40), a spirit of health being a good spirit and a goblin damned being, like Spenser's "damned sprights," one that would take advantage of a sick person's physical affliction and troubled soul. Later Hamlet affirms this reading when he says, "Out of my weakness and my melancholy," the devil, who "is very potent with such spirits [melancholy humour] / Abuses me to damn me" (II.ii.602-4). Today we note that depression leads to dark thoughts, but the Elizabethans mythologized the kind of depression that Hamlet is talking about. Lawrence Babb notes "the Devil's practice of victimizing melancholy men" because melancholy "is supposed to disorder the imagination greatly." And he cites Burton's statement on how sickness and melancholy provide an occasion for the devil to delude persons, as well as two further statements by Burton: the devil uses a melancholy person's weakness to tempt him to despair, and thus melancholy itself lures evil spirits.[18] In the *ars moriendi* tradition, then, a soul made unhealthy by sin ("ill" as evil) can disable the body, and an unhealthy body ("ill" as sick) renders the soul vulnerable to despair. As in the *ars moriendi* tradition, physical sickness and psychological/spiritual problems reinforce each other, with supernatural affliction as a frequent result.

Spenser's use of "ill" could be deliberately ambivalent, making the word mean sick as well as evil and enabling it to participate in a pattern of references throughout Book I to a mutually supportive relationship between poor health and a troubled mind and spirit.[19] Unlike the *moriens*, Redcrosse is not sick at the opening of the poem, but his melancholy, under the pressure of sin and imprisonment, ultimately becomes full-blown despair in Canto 9 at the hands of Despaire, who as a "man of hell" recalls the "damned sprights." From the very first stanzas of Book I, Redcrosse is on a course that reinforces the causal relationship between sin, sickness, and affliction by demons, and culminates in his *moriens*-like encounter with Despaire. His journey toward the episode that will most fully echo the *ars moriendi* tradition illustrates en route one of its principles.

At the very beginning of the story Spenser mentions that Redcrosse "of his cheere did seeme too solemne sad" (I.i.2). Clearly "the knight's natural bent appears to be toward melancholy. Spenser has much to say of the spiritual causes of despair, but he does not overlook its physiological and psychological origins."[20] After defeating Errour, Redcrosse is beset by Archimago, Satan's stand-in, who first uses a dream his sprites have fetched to try to deceive the knight. Quoting *Malleus Maleficarum*, Kerby Neill observes that "the devil, finding it difficult to attack the virtuous, 'molests them chiefly in dreams.'"[21]

When Archimago's stratagem fails, he uses demons to deceive Redcrosse visually with the lustful play of the supposed Una with a supposed knight at the beginning of Canto 2. This mythological event has a medical explanation: "A frequent result of melancholy, according to medical authorities, is hallucination."[22] Redcrosse then takes up with Duessa, who is of infernal lineage—the daughter of Deceit and Shame (I.v.26, 27), the granddaughter of Night (I.v.22), and the distant relative of Demogorgon (I.i.37, v.22), from whom all infernal figures in *The Faerie Queene* proceed.[23] At the House of Pride, Redcrosse confronts Sans Joy, the personification of his own melancholy nature, who is also part of the same demonic family tree. Although he defeats the pagan knight, he is wounded, is "not throughly heald" by the time he leaves, and later is "carelesse of his health" (I.v.45, vii.7).

Later still Redcrosse loses a battle with the giant Orgoglio and is thrown into a dungeon where his body and spirit waste away. Here is his physical condition when he is rescued by Arthur.

> His sad dull eyes deepe sunck in hollow pits,
> Could not endure th'vnwonted sunne to view;
> His bare thin cheekes for want of better bits,
> And empty sides deceiued of their dew,
> Could make a stony hart his hap to rew;
> His rawbone armes, whose mighty brawned bowrs
> Were wont to riue steele plates, and helmets hew,
> Were cleane consum'd, and all his vitall powres
> Decayd, and all his flesh shronk vp like withered flowres.
>   (I.viii.41)

Accordingly, Spenser calls Redcrosse "The chearelesse man, whom sorrow did dismay" (viii.43).

At the beginning of Canto 9 the knight encounters Sir Trevisan and questions him on his attempted suicide: "How may a man, said he, with idle speach / Be wonne, to spoyle the Castle of his health?" (ix.31), clearly echoing the title of Sir Thomas Elyot's *The Castle of Helthe* (1539). In *The Faerie Queene*, suicide is the ultimate negation of health. At this point, Redcrosse's condition is not much improved: he still has "shrunken synewes," and he is physically "weake and fraile" with such a horrified conscience that "all his manly powres it did disperse" (ix.20, 48-49). Melancholy and sin having brought his body low, Redcrosse now plays the role of the *moriens*, and sickness and guilt keep his soul in despair. The knight's suicidal tendencies persist even into the next canto: he has terrible pangs of conscience and "desirde to end his wretched dayes" (x.21). For Spenser's Elizabethan audience, these symptoms would have signaled extreme melancholy and the attendant temptation to suicide.[24] Indeed the literature of dying well nicely bears out the causal connection between illness and demon affliction. In a paragraph on sickness, for example, Caxton writes, "Fynallye, with the diuell, which than layith about him with all his engins and fals ties with helle, which than obiecteth and lay[i]th before hym the most vgly and dradfull furies."[25]

Redcrosse's physical debility, melancholy and despair signify a crippled spirit—what Burton would call religious melancholy as opposed to the joy a Christian should embrace.[26] But Spenser is careful to describe Redcrosse's state of mind and body in ways that would have signified to his Elizabethan readers an element of the *ars moriendi* tradition: the causal relationship between illness and demon affliction. Sickness and melancholy make him vulnerable to demons and to infernally predisposed characters throughout Book I. Being *ill* in this sense is a demon magnet in the Elizabethans' mythological understanding of human health. Thus Book I portrays Redcrosse as physically, psychologically, and spiritually sick, and the resulting assault by infernal forces culminates in his encounter with Despaire, the "man of hell," who plays the role of the demons in the *ars moriendi* tradition.

Much of the foregoing argument has been by inference, but there is one passage in Book I, not previously mentioned in connection with the art of dying, that explicitly supports the expanded definition of "ill" and the link between sickness and despair.[27] Even though demons are not present, the *moriens* can be

18

troubled by thoughts of damnation in hell, and so it is for Redcrosse in Canto 10. After his ordeal with Despaire, he goes to the House of Holiness for healing. At "an holy Hospitall" he finds seven "Bead-men," who take care of other people's physical needs (x.36). By stressing the psychological difficulty faced by the sick and dying, Spenser squarely aligns with the *ars moriendi* tradition and illustrates the causal relationship between body and soul.

> The fift had charge sicke persons to attend,
> And comfort those, in point of death which lay;
> For them most needeth comfort in the end,
> When sin, and hell, and death do most dismay
> The feeble soule departing hence away.
> All is but lost, that liuing we bestow,
> If not well ended at our dying day.
> O man haue mind of that last bitter throw;
> For as the tree does fall, so lyes it euer low. (I.x.41)

It follows that modern editors are only partially correct about the meaning of "ill men." To be sure, Despaire plays rhetorical tricks and flashes a picture of torment in hell ("ill" as evil), but physical weakness is present in the Despaire episode: illness, as illness, makes Redcrosse vulnerable. He is predisposed to despair by his physical and psychological condition, and his state of mind and body is a further connection to the *ars moriendi* tradition. Sin and illness are mutually reinforcing: sin leads to physical illness, which in turn makes him vulnerable to further sin (despair, suicide) and to supernatural affliction. Thus his insufficient reaction to Despaire makes dramatic sense because the encounter is the culmination of a downward movement that one can chart with respect to his physical condition. In Canto 9 he is momentarily one of the "ill men," both sinful and sick, whom Despaire, the "man of hell," makes "aghast."

2. Theology and the *Ars Moriendi* in Cantos 9 and 10

When applied to the Despaire episode, how do the *ars moriendi* tradition and general eschatology illuminate the theology of *The Faerie Queene*? The conventional wisdom is Virgil K. Whitaker's statement that the episode is "staunch Protestantism," with Despaire's argument reading "like a deliberate imitation of Calvinist statements on human depravity."[28] But the *ars moriendi* was a Catholic phenomenon, originating in the Middle Ages with "macabre extravagances" designed to motivate people to submit to Roman Catholic authority. Even in the *ars moriendi* books of Spenser's time, we are told, Catholics emphasize judgment and hell whereas Protestants devote greater attention to "heaven as the final reward for the prepared Christian."[29] In light of this distinction, Canto 9 may reflect a Catholic eschatology. Despaire stresses both judgment and hell—"the greater sin, the greater punishment" (43)—and nowhere are they more apparent than in his use of the imagery of eternal torment in hell in stanza 49.

> To driue him to despaire, and quite to quaile,
> He shew'd him painted in a table plaine,
> The damned ghosts, that doe in torments waile,
> And thousand feends that doe them endlesse paine
> With fire and brimstone, which for euer shall remaine.

Despaire's emphasis on judgment and the torments of hell is not necessarily an echo of Calvinist harshness; it may simply harken back to the Catholicism of the Middle Ages and in particular to priests' attempts to maintain authority over their parishoners.

My purpose is to use the *ars moriendi* to chart "theological distinctions" that will illuminate the Despaire and House of Holiness episodes.[30] Some clarification of terms is necessary at the outset. John N. King and Carol Kaske emphasize the unity of Protestant thought in Spenser's age as opposed to the distinction often emphasized between the Puritans and the Church of England.[31] For King there was "a broad consensus concerning official theology," but eschatology does include a distinction between Protestant points of view that is relevant to the Despaire episode.

Here is the distinction, for which I am indebted to John F. H. New, that bears upon the difference between Despaire's emphasis on justice and Una's reminder of grace. Of course, New's use of the term "Anglican" is anachronistic, but his point is an important one.

> The Puritans expected unremitting severity on Judgment Day, whereas Anglicans looked forward to leniency. . . . Anglicanism was not universalistic, neither did Puritanism expect universal reprobation. Furthermore, the ideas about the Last Judgment were less matters of dogma than dispositions of mind. Nevertheless, if we keep these difficulties and reservations in view, we may yet characterize the two eschatologies as mercy versus impartial justice, joy versus condemnation, and subjective optimism versus an objective pessimism.[32]

If New is right that the Puritans are to the Church of England as justice is to mercy, then how did mainstream Protestants reconcile mercy with the doctrine of predestination, and what role does predestination play in the Despaire episode?

I agree fully with Kaske that predestination is clearly present; indeed it is the crux of both Despaire's argument and Una's reply.[33] Despaire's point is that Redcrosse is one of the reprobate, predestined to hell "by righteous sentence of th'Almighties law" (50). Una argues, on the other hand, that being among the elect he is predestined to heaven: "In heauenly mercies hast thou not a part? / Why shouldst thou then despeire, that chosen art?" (ix.53). The issue of predestination is fundamental to Canto 9, for overmuch contemplation on the issue leads to despair, which is in turn "the special temptation of God's elect" and can lead to suicide.[34]

According to Darryl J. Gless, "Elizabethan orthodoxy could appear to include the doctrine of double predestination, which (as Calvin explains) views both salvation and damnation as direct functions of divine will." For example, Article XVII states that God will "deliver from curse and damnation [only] those whom He hath chosen in Christ out of mankind."[35] This binary implication gave rise to a controversy that illuminates the debate in Canto 9. How can a merciful God predestine people to damnation? The question is irrelevant if "Spenser does not go so far as the . . . doctrine of predestination unto damnation,"[36] but that doctrine is certainly present in Despaire's rhetoric. New begins by stating that "Anglicanism solved the problem by assuming there was a scale, or gradation, of torments in Hell." In support, he quotes John Pearson and Hugh Latimer.[37] Pearson writes in *An Exposition of the Creed*, "'It is absolutely necessary . . . to believe that a just and exact retribution is defined, that a due and proportionable dispensation of rewards and punishments is reserved to another world.'" Pearson also writes "that the Punishment which shall be inflicted on them [the wicked] shall be proportionate to their Sins, as a Recompence of their Demerits, so that no Man shall suffer more than he hath deserved."[38] New quotes Latimer's *Sermons* as identifying "'three degrees of punishments'; 'for the greater the sin is, the greater is the punishment in hell.'" Latimer's statement directly anticipates Despaire's rhetoric: "The lenger life, I wote the greater sin, / The greater sin, the greater punishment."

One does not need to call Despaire's argument Puritan to account for his statement on the supposed damnation that awaits Redcrosse. His statement to Redcrosse is actually consistent with official Church of England theology, which claims that predestination and mercy are compatible through the gradations of torment to which Despaire refers. The notion of damnation does not contradict God's mercy if one views gradations in punishment as a manifestation of divine mercy. Both Despaire and Una argue within a Calvinist context, but Canto 9 puts a distinctively Church of England spin on the Calvinist doctrine of predestination insofar as God's mercy qualifies the eternal damnation of the reprobate. Despaire, one of the great enemies of holiness, is insidiously effective through his adept use of a mainstream theological concept to present suicide as a positive option.

Whereas Canto 9 emphasizes death, Canto 10 emphasizes life, and the shift reflects a development in the *ars moriendi* tradition. Over time, the *ars moriendi* takes on some of the characteristics of the *ars vivendi*: if a person wants to die well, he must live well, for a good life is the best preparation for a holy death—"so that if you liue wel, you shal dye wel."[39] The Redcrosse knight's visit to the House of Holiness illustrates not only this convergence of the arts of dying and living well but also the theological mixture within Spenser's use of the *ars moriendi*. Whereas the Despaire episode strongly reflects the Church of England's theology while seeming to incorporate Puritan and even Medieval Catholic elements, the House of Holiness episode, though it incorporates Catholic figures and conventions, includes a culmination that is strikingly Protestant in light of the *ars moriendi* tradition.

To begin with, numerous elements of the *ars moriendi* tradition merge with the *ars vivendi*. We see, first, Redcrosse receiving instruction in faith, hope, patience, charity, humility, zeal, and reverence—correctives for his desperate condition after the encounter with Despaire but prescriptions for right living as well. Personified, these qualities are exactly opposite the five deathbed temptations:

- unbelief vs. Fidelia (4, 12-13)
- despair vs. Speranza (4, 14), Zele (6)
- impatience vs. Patience (23)
- vainglory vs. Humiltá (5), Reuerence (7)
- avarice vs. Charissa (4)

Redcrosse does what Perkins prescribes: "When men do make the right vse of their afflictions, wither they bee in body or mind or both, and do with al their might indeuour to beare them patiently, humbling themselues as vnder the correction of God, then they begin to die well."[40]

If to live well is to prepare to die well, then so far Canto 10 illustrates the link between the art of dying and the art of living, for at the House of Holiness Redcrosse encounters the personifications of the exact qualities that one must manifest on the deathbed. Such instruction is crucial because the knight sorely needs healing: he still has "dull eyes," dullness being a sign of enduring melancholy (18); as noted above, he remains suicidal (21); he continues to suffer "that disease of grieued conscience" (23); his "inward corruption, and infected sin / . . . behind remained still, / And festring sore did rankle yet within" (25); and his "proud humors" remain awash in his veins (26). He is still an "ill" man in the medical sense, physically and psychologically debilitated, but receives tutoring in the proper spiritual orientation, much as good counselors help the *moriens* focus on positive things. Nancy Lee Beaty sums up these points in a comment on the tradition in general: "True friends should urge the sick to contrition and confession; and . . . this may improve his bodily health as well."[41] Just so, the House of Holiness provides spiritual healing, from which will proceed improved physical health, the allegorical representation of sound spirituality. One recalls the earlier-quoted statement about the illogic of calling the physician before the priest: Spenser would agree that spiritual healing must precede physical healing.

Despite numerous Catholic motifs, the House of Holiness episode culminates in what should be viewed as a Protestant element of the *ars moriendi* tradition. As for Catholicism, Spenser mentions "ashes and sack cloth" (26), penance (27), and the seven beadsmen. Whitaker states that stanzas 38 (alms giving) and 51 (what Redcrosse can do "his sinfull soule to saue") imply "that works have 'merit.'" So far the episode bears out Whitaker's sense that "the substance of Canto 10 is Catholic in origin," yet, as Robert L. Reid observes, Fidelia's initiation of the healing process, her giving the keys to the kingdom of heaven to Contemplation, and the emphasis on Patience (an "inner response rather than priestly authority") indicate "the staunch Protestantism of this part of the allegory."[42] In addition, the knight's vision of the New Jerusalem participates in a distinctly Protestant element of the House of Holiness episode. Redcrosse learns that his "dwellynge [will be] in heuynly Ierusalem euerlastyngly"[43] and that he will become St. George (x.61). Seeing is believing, and the vision on the Mount of Contemplation provides ocular proof that he is "chosen" and "ordaind a blessed end" (57, 61). Here in the doctrine of predestination is the logical culmination of Una's argument in Canto 9, stanza 53. The object of the vision—the "new *Hierusalem*" (57)—is mentioned in the *ars moriendi* literature. In Becon, for example, Philemon counsels his dying friend Epaphroditus with a description of the heavenly city: "In thys worlde we all are but strangers & pelgrimes. We haue here no dwelling citie, but looke for an other that is to come."[44] But now the point for Redcrosse is that assurance takes on the force of a deathbed vision. Una's argument in Canto 9 helps the knight understand that he is among the elect,[45] and now the vision, the ultimate inoculation against despair, cements his belief. Like a soul that flits away to experience a foretaste of heaven, Redcrosse can now view his own afterlife with confidence. David Lee Cressy quotes such a story from the year 1661: "Almost delirious as he passed away, Searle told his tutor, 'he had been twice in heaven since his sickness', and when assured 'we should meet in heaven, had answered, that we should be joyful indeed.'"[46] So it is not that the vision signals that Redcrosse has already become a saint but that the vision confirms a Protestant sense of his ultimate destination.[47]

Here, then, is how Spenser's *ars moriendi* works in the House of Holiness episode: a proper spiritual orientation leads to bodily health and good deeds; faith, health, and works are in a mutually reinforcing relationship with the vision of the New Jerusalem. The result is like the return from what Carol Zaleski calls the otherworld journey—"those who return from the other world are never the same again"; or as Drythelm puts it, "'from now on I must live not according to my old habits, but in a much different manner.'"[48] Redcrosse's vision (like Adam's in *Paradise Lost*) is an essential part of his knightly journey toward Protestant holiness. Redcrosse is now an image of "Everyman as independent Protestant."[49] Confidence in his own salvation is something that arises from his individual spiritual experience, not through the mediation of the Church, for heavenly vision is proof of future salvation. The Beadsmen help him, but ultimately he transcends their ministrations. Therefore, as Eric R. Seeman writes, the vision resolves the "tension between predestinarian teachings and people's desire for assurance that they were saved," and enables an inversion of the power dynamic between clergy and laity.[50] Of course, Seeman is writing about deathbed experiences in New England where all persons are presumably Protestant to begin with, yet his ideas also hold for the distinctively Protestant quality of Redcrosse's experience.

In terms of the individual's assertion of certainty without church authority, if layman is to clergy as the Protestant church is to the Roman Catholic Church, the knight's progress at the House of Holiness suggests the historical allegory that Spenser mentions in the Letter to Ralegh: the journey of Holiness from the Catholic Church's direct ministrations in the life of a believer to the distinctly individual and Protestant conviction of salvation without the mediation of church authority. Spenser "contradicts himself irreconcilably" on free will and justification and creates "ever-dilating outlines" within the the House of Holiness episode[51] only if it is assumed that he is attempting to allegorize a consistent theological position. But the contradiction disappears if the episode is viewed as an allegory of holiness over the centuries. By the time he leaves the House of Holiness, Redcrosse confidently represents the Protestant Christian who is well equipped to avoid despair and the resulting damnation in hell because he now knows beyond doubt that "death is nothing else but . . . an ending of exile . . . turning again into his country; and entering into bliss and joy."[52]

3. The *Ars Moriendi* and Guyon's "Like Race"

The connection between the Redcrosse knight's encounter with Despaire and his visit to the House of Holiness, as well as numerous elements thoughout the book, indicates that Spenser's use of the *ars moriendi* tradition is not merely a reference point for a single episode. If we take the analogy one step further, the question is whether the tradition informs anything in Book II. If Guyon's journey is a "like race to runne" (II.i.32), what episode corresponds to Redcrosse's encounter with Despaire and why? Hamilton writes, "The senseless Redcross knight dominated by Orgoglio is an emblem of the total depravity of human nature, the death of the spirit," and "Guyon, prostrate upon the ground under the wrathful Pyrochles and the lustful Cymochles, is an emblem of man's body dominated by the irascible and concupiscent affections."[53] Redcrosse in the dungeon parallels the unconscious Guyon insofar as each situation represents a fall. Hamilton vaguely suggests that Redcrosse's inability to slay Despaire parallels Guyon's inability to slay Furor and Disdain (in each case, the insufficiency of natural virtue is on display) and virtually skips from Orgoglio to the House of Holiness. In contrast, John Erskine Hankins identifies the caves of Despaire and Mammon as parallel testing places.[54] Both critics, of course, are making important points: Hamilton emphasizes the perils of the flesh; Hankins, of the devil. The *ars moriendi* tradition, however, suggests a parallel between Redcrosse's negative reaction to Despaire and Guyon's faint.

Spenser's phrase is first of all an echo of the *ars moriendi*: for example, Becon's Epaphroditus (echoing Paul's statement about his own coming death in 2 Timothy 4:7) says, "I haue runne my race."[55] If "race" means "the course of life or some portion of it,"[56] Spenser's phrase means that Guyon's overall life parallels Redcrosse's in meaningful ways, not merely that specific elements of their recorded journeys reflect each other. If "death is sleep's counterpart which we put on daily like a garment,"[57] then Guyon's faint emerges as the equivalent of Redcrosse's near encounter with death in the Despaire episode. As in the *ars moriendi* tradition, the knight is protected by an angel from the assault of Pyrochles, who, like Despaire, is a man of hell insofar as Spenser associates anger with hell-pain (II.vi.44, 50). But more significantly, the episode calls to mind "The angel's good inspiration against despair," which shows Saul and his horse sprawled at the foot of the dying man's bed. Although Saul is probably conscious, both he and Guyon are prostrate on the ground. The Saul image suggests not only the forgiveness of great sins but also the idea of transition to (greater) Christian faith. The Despaire canto and Guyon's faint echo this transition. Redcrosse's encounter with Despaire is the knight's final attempt to solve his spiritual problems without the aid of grace, and he soon develops a proper spiritual orientation at the House of Holiness. Guyon's faint and the angel's protection mark his transition from classical to Christian temperance (one of the subjects addressed in Chapter Three).

The 1590 poem concludes with the poet's intention to rest on the sabbath; since Spenser intends to continue the poem, the sense of death's finality is postponed. The last word on death in *The Faerie Queene* concerns Spenser's own; in fact, it is on this note that *The Two Cantos of Mutabilitie* (1609) conclude:

> Then gin I thinke on that which Nature sayd,
> Of that same time when no more *Change* shall be,
> But stedfast rest of all things firmely stayd
>
> Upon the pillours of Eternity,
> That is contrayr to *Mutabilitie*:
> For, all that moueth, doth in *Change* delight:
> But thence-forth all shall rest eternally
> With Him that is the God of Sabbaoth hight:
> O! that great Sabbaoth God, grant me that Sabaoths sight. (xiii.2)

The stanza reverses the negative dimensions of rest in Book I: Redcrosse's dereliction of duty when he disarms and dallies with Duessa, and Despaire's argument that the knight can achieve "sleepe after toyle, port after stormie seas, / Ease after warre," if he will "but here lie downe, and to thy rest betake" (ix.40, 44). The final line echoes the hopeful uncertainty of the *moriens* who has not had the benefit of Redcrosse's otherworld vision, but Spenser's meditation on his own death does participate in the nexus of the art of dying and the art of living. As one of the elect, he has not earned salvation, but his life of duty as public servant and poet has been excellent preparation for a peaceful departure.

CHAPTER TWO

THESEUS AS HARROWER OF HELL IN BOOK I

Chapter Two explores the legend of Theseus in much the same way as Chapter One explores the *ars moriendi*, as an extended analogy.[1] The role of myth in the underworld of Book I will prove as crucial to interpretation as the aid of Theseus proverbially was to difficult situations. As Plutarch explains:

> Albeit in his time other princes of Greece had done many goodly and notable exploits in the warres, yet Herodotus is of opinion, that Theseus was never in any one of them: saving that he was at the battell of the Lapithae against the Centauri. Others saye to the contrarie, that he was at the jorney of Cholchide with Iason, and that he dyd helpe Meleager to kill the wilde bore of Calydonia: from whence (as they saye) this proverbe came: 'Not without Theseus.' Meaning that such a thing was not done without great helpe of another.[2]

Like difficult tasks in classical myth, an interpretation of the Redcrosse knight's experiences in Book I of *The Faerie Queene* must also be "Not without Theseus." Spenser's allusions to the Cretan labyrinth in Canto 1 and less explicitly in Canto 4, Theseus's condemnation "to endlesse slouth by law" (v.35),[3] the retelling of the Hippolytus story (v.36-40), and other elements of the Theseus myth show that Spenser made more careful use of this material—in parallels as well as at points of divergence in setting, plot, characterization, and theme—than has been previously understood. But the Theseus myth has deeper significance for a reading of Book I than a simple Theseus-Redcrosse analogy would suggest. As a natural man whose moral decay contrasts with the spiritual improvement that a Protestant knight must achieve, Theseus provides a negative gloss on Redcrosse's journey to mature holiness. By indicting Redcrosse yet highlighting his spiritual progress, the diverse elements in the life of Theseus enable a new reading of key episodes.

1. Labyrinth, Wood, and Cave

Spenser's statement in *The Ruines of Rome* (1591) that "Crete will boast the labyrinth" (line 21) nicely demonstrates the presence of Crete in his thinking about the labyrinth around the time the first three books of *The Faerie Queene* were published. Indeed, the underworld of Book I relates to Theseus's defeat of the Minotaur in the Cretan labyrinth, which prefigures and contrasts with his later unsuccessful attempt with his friend Pirithous to abduct Persephone from hell. Since Errour is encountered in a labyrinthine structure, the labyrinths of ancient myth, especially the archetypal one of the Minotaur, can illuminate Spenser's more modern myth.[4] Given the widely ranging citations found in Spenser criticism, it appears that archeologists are divided on whether the Cretan labyrinth was unicursal (a single, convoluted path leading to the center) or multicursal (with alternate routes, dead ends, or both).[5] Angus Fletcher states that "there are no blind alleys in the pure Cretan design," meaning that it is unicursal. But since a unicursal labyrinth obviates the need for a ball of thread, William Blissett seems right to say that the Cretan labyrinth is multicursal and "shows the curious anomaly of being *experienced* as unicursal on the way in and multicursal on the way out" (my emphasis).[6]

Rather than being wholly unicursal or multicursal, the wood of error, where "all within were pathes and alleies wide" (i.7), combines a key element of each pattern. Soon Redcrosse, Una, and the dwarf lose their way in the multicursal wood and cannot find their chosen path:

> Led with delight, they thus beguile the way,
> Vntill the blustring storme is ouerblowne;
> When weening to returne, whence they did stray,
> They cannot finde that path, which first was showne,

> But wander too and fro in wayes vnknowne,
> Furthest from end then, when they neerest weene,
> That makes them doubt, their wits be not their owne:
> So many pathes, so many turnings seene,
> That which of them to take, in diuerse doubt they been. (10)

Then, in an attempt to resume their direction, they take the beaten path—"That path they take, that beaten seemd most bare, / And like to lead the labyrinth about"—which "brought them to a hollow caue, / Amid the thickest woods" (11). After Redcrosse kills Errour, he and his companions take the same broad path out of the wood:

> Then mounted he vpon his Steede againe,
> And with the Lady backward sought to wend;
> That path he kept, which beaten was most plaine,
> Ne euer would to any by-way bend,
> But still did follow one vnto the end,
> The which at last out of the wood them brought. (28)

As this brief account reveals, Spenser's labyrinth combines unicursal and multicursal features. While there is clearly more than one path to choose from, a main path leads to the cave, and it is the same path that Redcrosse and his companions follow to reach Errour's den and later to leave the wood.

Spenser's conflation of labyrinth types reflects the nature of error and foreshadows subsequent events. Once a person enters a state of error (the wood), two types of wrong path are possible: small ones whose meanderings disorient a walker, and large ones leading more directly to a confrontation with a Minotaur-figure, which represents one's sinful self and the potential for self-ruin. Although resulting in a victory, the encounter with Errour ironically heralds error later on, and Redcrosse will make errors both small and large. Ignoring Fradubio's warning about Fidessa/Duessa is a small mistake, while following "a broad high way" straight to the House of Pride reveals serious shortcomings (iv.2). But despite the imagery of the broad road that Spenser employs throughout the book, the knight's path, which resembles the wood of error in being full of choices, contains the multicursal "by-way[s]" mentioned in Canto 1, stanza 28. Therefore, the possibility of choice in a multicursal life affirms a Christian rather than classical view: free will to choose the one right path versus a fixed fate.[7]

Offering a choice of direction, Canto 1's labyrinthine wood is a fitting emblem to introduce the journey of a Christian knight, and its structure sums up a truth about bad choices of direction along the way. The world in which Redcrosse journeys is a labyrinth encompassing smaller labyrinths, which correspond to individual challenges that must be met and overcome. Redcrosse enters error/sin easily, encounters opponents representing his own sinful nature, and retraces his steps with varying degrees of difficulty: approach, encounter, and extrication. As Theseus must retrace his steps to escape the labyrinth, so Redcrosse must reverse the consequences of error through amendment, penance, remorse, and repentance at the House of Holiness. Getting out of a labyrinth, whether it be a physical structure or a moral condition, involves more than having a change of heart.

Like Errour's den, other caves in *The Faerie Queene* are labyrinthine either in structure or in function. Although *labyrinth* and *maze* have nearly identical definitions in the *OED*,[8] the etymology of the former supports the theory that the site mythologized as the Cretan labyrinth is within the earth. Whereas *maze* derives from such Old English words as *mase* and relates to the modern English *amazed* (a connection to the disorientation experienced within a maze-like structure, as in stanza 10 above), *labyrinth*, a transliteration through Latin of the Greek λαβύρινθος, means "place of stone."[9] Accordingly, in one version of the Theseus myth, the Minotaur lived in a cave in the mountains, or land of labyrinths,[10] and one theory holds that the origin of the Cretan labyrinth was the Gortyna Cavern's "remarkable series of winding passages" within Mount Ida on the southern side of Crete.[11]

Errour's cave and Despaire's cave (ix.33, 35), two settings not ordinarily considered together, thus emerge as aspects of a labyrinth topos uniting the key episodes of Book I. Whereas Errour's cave dwelling parallels the center of the maze where the Minotaur dwells, the cave in Canto 9 resembles a labyrinth as a kind of tomb.[12] Like the Minotaur's bloody residence, Despaire's cave craves bodies, and the surrounding area is rife with the imagery of death: it is "an hollow caue, / Farre vnderneath a craggie clift ypight, / Darke, dolefull, drearie, like a greedie graue, / That still for carrion carcases doth craue," and many "carcases" lie "scattered on the greene" (ix.33, 34). Whereas Redcrosse drags Errour toward the light of day, he encounters Despaire on his own territory, allowing him to dictate the terms of discourse: "That darkesome caue they enter, where they find / That cursed man, low sitting on the ground" (ix.35). The contrast suggests that the knight has gone from defeating Errour in heroic fashion, much as Theseus slays the Minotaur, to being like one of the sacrificial youths condemned to death in the labyrinth as a tribute to King Minos, helpless to do anything except suffer his fate. To encounter error one must be active, but despair is a passive state. Far along on the broad road introduced in Canto 1, Redcrosse now abandons his initial desire to try the "treachours art" (ix.32) as if he were an avenger and experiences instead the passive despair of a sacrificial victim.

2. Ariadne and Una

Yet that Redcrosse in Canto 1 is a Theseus-figure and not a victim is clear from Una's Ariadne-like role in Canto 1.[13] In the myth, Theseus has not only a ball of thread but also a ball of pitch, which he jams into the Minotaur's mouth to prevent the monster from biting him. In medieval allegory, the story of Theseus in the labyrinth parallels Christ's harrowing of hell, with the pitch analogous to Christ's humanity, and the thread analogous to his divinity.[14] More recently, the thread has been allegorized as human sympaty and as reason.[15] In *The Faerie Queene*, Ariadne's thread is a metaphor signifying something natural or supernatural that helps one out of a tight spot. Una cries out, "Add faith vnto your force, and be not faint: / Strangle her, else she sure will strangle thee" (I.i.19). Certainly the violent imagery recalls what Theseus must do to the Minotaur. And

34

Una's cry is not only a reminder of faith in God but also a manifestation of love both human and divine. Redcrosse and Una, after all, are to be betrothed, much as Ariadne falls deeply in love with Theseus. The theme of love receives support from the following Christian adaptation of the Theseus myth, in which love is both human and divine. A small maze in the cathedral at Lucca, Italy, which was built in the 11th to 13th centuries, bears a Latin inscription that reads, "This is the labyrinth which the Cretan Daedalus built, out of which nobody could get who was inside, except Theseus; nor could he have done it, unless he had been helped with a thread by Ariadne, all for love."[16] On the one hand, the inscription celebrates love on the human level between man and woman; on the other, its cathedral setting implies God's love as actual grace, which helps persons out of difficult situations. In a similar way, the knight's faith, an inner response to God's love as prevenient grace, makes possible a synergy of faith and force in his victory over Errour. Immediately after Una cries out, Redcrosse makes progress in the fight:

> That when he heard, in great perplexitie,
> His gall did grate for griefe and high disdaine,
> And knitting all his force got one hand free,
> Wherewith he grypt her gorge with so great paine,
> That soone to loose her wicked bands did her constraine. (19)

While describing victory, this stanza also conveys Redcrosse's spiritual immaturity. He may begin to make progress against Errour not because he adds faith to his force but because the "high disdaine" he feels is for his martial incompetence or his carnal self rather than the monster, or because, on a purely instinctive level, he fears strangulation. A nontheological view of the battle receives support from stanza 24:

> Thus ill bestedd, and fearefull more of shame,
> Then of the certaine perill he stood in,
> Halfe furious vnto his foe he came,
> Resolv'd in minde all suddenly to win,
> Or soone to lose, before he once would lin;
> And strooke at her with more then manly force.

Although his "more then manly force" supports the idea that faith has made the power of grace active in the battle, the knight's newfound strength may stem instead from the fear of shame or from fury—anger at his foe or, worse yet, at himself for revealing his incompetence in arms to a woman (or, allegorically, his inexperience in faith to the True Church). Redcrosse may also fear the sexual pollution Errour represents. She is, after all, an analogue to the Minotaur, which springs from and embodies the unrestrained lust of Pasiphae and the bull. Thus, along with being a positive response to the human and divine love that corresponds to Ariadne's thread, Redcrosse's defeat of Errour may illustrate a negative connection to himself—the very concupiscible and irascible passions that characterize Theseus's violent and criminal behavior in his later life.

Like Theseus's victory over the Minotaur, Redcrosse's defeat of Errour conveys a sense of impending error, of which the abandonment of a woman is the best example: as Theseus selfishly abandons Ariadne on the isle of Naxos, Redcrosse self-righteously leaves the sleeping Una at Archimago's hermitage and takes up with Fidessa/Duessa. Less obvious is that the parallel between Ariadne and Una continues into their respective wanderings and indicts Redcrosse. Ariadne is befriended by Bacchus. The contemporary view, which associates the god of wine with drunkenness and unrestrained revelry, does not pertain to *The Faerie Queene*. Whereas overindulgence causes drunkenness, wine properly used has a "civilizing influence,"[17] and Spenser's view of Bacchus is highly positive:

> But euermore some of the vertuous race
> Rose vp, inspired with heroicke heat,
> That cropt the branches of the sient base,
> And with strong hand their fruitfull rancknes did deface.

> Such first was *Bacchus*, that with furious might
> All th'East before vntam'd did ouerronne,
> And wrong repressed, and establisht right,
> Which lawlesse men had formerly fordonne.
> There Iustice first her princely rule begonne. (V.i.1-2)

As a figure of justice and a righter of wrongs, Bacchus, who marries the faithful

Ariadne and makes her his queen, parallels the lion, which in Canto 3 becomes Una's protector in recognition of the Truth she represents ("*Forsaken Truth long seekes her loue, / And makes the Lyon mylde*," Spenser writes in his synopsis of Canto 3). The parallel between Ariadne and Una (as the True Church) is strengthened by *Ovide Moralisé*: Bacchus (God) will comfort Ariadne (the Church) and make her his spouse and friend.[18] Of course, the point is not that Spenser's lion represents God; rather the lion represents England and, as H. S. V. Jones points out, the law of nature,[19] which support the True Church; Bacchus and the lion thus become structural parallels by aiding a woman in need.

The difference between Una and Ariadne is equally significant for Spenser: unlike Ariadne who embraces her new surroundings, Una declines the earthly privilege offered by the Satyrs—the "woodborne people" who "fall before her flat, / And worship her as Goddesse of the wood" (vi.16). By refusing to be worshipped or made "th'Image of Idolatryes" (19), Una justifies Spenser's earlier comparison of her to Odysseus: she follows "wayes vnknowne, her wandring knight to seeke, / With paines farre passing that long wandring *Greeke*, / That for his loue refused deitie" (iii.21). Refusing to assume a position of deity/royalty breaks the parallel to Ariadne. Instead of staying in the mythic realm of fauns and satyrs who confuse "the phenomenal with the transcendent,"[20] or the signifying woman/church with the signified Truth, Una leaves the woodland folk as Odysseus leaves Calypso. The poet, then, uses classical allusion to affirm the purpose Redcrosse easily forgets but will remember, the quest to bring aid to captive Eden. As they journey through Book I, both Redcrosse and Una will move outward from encounters with such figures as Errour and the Satyrs, whose classical antecedents underscore human error, toward episodes that affirm Christian duty and manifest the potential for spiritual growth. As Una breaks the parallel to Ariadne, so Redcrosse, as we shall see, breaks the parallel to Theseus in ways that mark his spiritual progress.

3. The Minotaur and Errour

The Theseus of classical myth, though he plays a large number of roles, is most famous in the world-as-labyrinth for slaying the Minotaur, which parallels Errour in several ways. Although neither monster travels beyond a labyrinthine setting, both have impact abroad. As error pervades the landscape of Book I, every ninth year Athens must send a tribute to King Minos in Crete—seven youths and seven maidens who are thrown into the labyrinth, either to be killed by the Minotaur or to lose their way and die. Moreover, both creatures are unnatural, mingling elements that the hero must negotiate later on. Being the product of Pasiphae's lust for a bull and having the head of a bull and the body of a man, the Minotaur represents the life-long struggle within Theseus himself between the threat of unrestrained passion and the potential for reasonable self-control—the bestial versus the human. To emphasize this point, Plutarch quotes Euripides's description of the Minotaur: "A corps combynd, which monstrous might be deemd: / A Boye, a Bull, both man and beast it seemd."[21] As in a dream, man and bull (the Minotaur) or woman and dragon (Errour) are condensed into a single image, so that both creatures are metaphors that prefigure the challenges the heroes must overcome.

Since myth expresses the contents of the unconscious, which the labyrinth image frequently symbolizes,[22] Theseus and Redcrosse are battling its two main instincts: eros (each monster's human part, which foreshadows crimes against women in the Theseus myth and sins with Duessa in Book I)[23] and thanatos (the reptile/bestial part, which heralds murderous behavior in the Theseus myth and the dragon in Spenser). As regards instinct, Theseus functions much like a deity in Freud's analysis of myth, in which "the gods are granted the satisfaction of all the desires which human creatures have to renounce . . . a human desire is transformed into a divine privilege. But in the legend the deity possesses nothing of the characteristics of a super-ego: he is still the representative of the paramount life of the instincts."[24] The god is assigned the role of the unrestrained id, and so, I would argue, is Theseus. Despite a civilizing role as leader of Athens, which suggests superego or Minos-like law, his life is a catalog of unrestrained lust and violence emanating from the id. Eros and thanatos even unite in his war with the Amazons, violence being bound up with conflicting desires for two women, the Amazon Hippolyta and Ariadne's sister, Phaedra. In other words, Theseus's id proves too strong for an ego unsupported by the Christian faith. As a manifestation of primitive instinct, Theseus represents the shortcomings of the Redcrosse knight in Canto 1, but whereas the two heroes are at a similar stage of psychic development in the battle with the Minotaur or Errour, Theseus is static, Redcrosse dynamic, in dealing with unconscious drives. The victory over Errour marks the knight's problems, but the victory over the dragon reveals his progress.

The slaying of Errour is a victory that reveals Redcrosse's initial shortcomings when he is viewed not as Theseus but in other terms that the myth provides. The labyrinth is an appropriate setting for a victory that is a not-victory because "the concept of *aporia* (the 'unpassable path,' self-contradiction, paradox) sheds light on the labyrinth's embodiment of paradox, its simultaneous affirmation of antinomies: order/chaos, imprisonment/liberation, linearity/circularity, clarity/complexity, stability/instability."[25] Redcrosse is a victor in Canto 1 and a victim, like Athens's sacrificial youths, in Canto 9, but he also plays both of these roles in the Errour episode. The historical basis of the sacrificial youths supports a qualified view of the knight's adventure in the wood. Rather than being sent to Crete, as Plutarch says, to atone for the death of King Minos's eldest son,[26] Athenian youths may have travelled there on their own, gotten into serious trouble and been forced to take part in bull-jumping games or sacrificed in some other way.[27] Youth is responsible for its own inextricable, labyrinthine troubles, much as Redcrosse foolishly engages a foe more than his equal.

The functions of ancient labyrinths also help bring the knight's error into focus. One ordinarily thinks of a labyrinth as a place designed to entrap, but "a labyrinth has only as a secondary implication the danger of getting lost inside it; the primary and essential quality is the power to obstruct entry, but also to allow it on proper terms." The latter function characterizes a "tactical labyrinth," one designed to "exclude the unfriendly, and yet when necessary to admit the friendly."[28] What happens to interpretation if the labyrinthine wood in Canto 1 is designed not to lead a walker into error but to make the state of error difficult to enter? Although the beaten path that winds through the wood echoes the broad and easy way to destruction and contrasts with the straight and narrow way,[29] the "many pathes" and "turnings" that Redcrosse and his companions encounter once they leave the main road are not meant to lead them straight to the cave. The broad path must not be easy to follow, since they go astray on lesser tracks. It is only by an act of will in stanza 11—"At last resoluing forward still to fare, / Till that some end they finde or in or out, / That path they take, that beaten seemd most bare"—that they arrive at Errour's cave. Similarly, the battle results not from any attack by the monster but instead from Redcrosse's own overconfidence. After Una warns him that they have reached Errour's den, his reaction is worthy of the young persons who go astray on Crete:

> But full of fire and greedy hardiment,
> The youthfull knight could not for ought be staide,
> But forth vnto the darksome hole he went,
> And looked in. (14)

Errour's reaction, once she sees the mail-clad knight, is to flee back into her cave, as if she just wants to be left alone:

> She lookt about, and seeing one in mayle
> Armed to point, sought backe to turne againe;
> For light she hated as the deadly bale,
> Ay wont in desert darknesse to remaine,
> Where plaine none might her see, nor she see any plaine. (16)

Then "the valiant Elfe . . . her boldly kept / From turning backe" (17). Although action is just what is needed in the narrative sense, his allegorical error, like that of Theseus, is the attempt to solve a spiritual problem with psychological or physical force—the same error that Redcrosse commits when he fights Sans Joy at the House of Pride and again when he tries to slay and match wits with Despaire. But these passages also suggest that Redcrosse is less a Theseus-figure who wins an effortless victory over a Minotaur-figure than an upstart youth who, like those in trouble on Crete, brings a labyrinth of problems on himself. Rather than being, as Spenser implies in stanza 16, an exemplum of how a man worthy of praise may defeat error by exposing it to the light, the episode reveals the Redcrosse knight's dogged determination to go astray and the same retrograde motion found in Jeremiah 7:24: "But thei wolde not obey, nor incline their eare, but went after the counsels and the stubbernes of their wicked heart, & went backewarde and not forwarde."

4. The Labyrinthine Underworld and the House of Pride

If parts of Book I lacking explicit mention of Theseus can be fruitfully interpreted in light of the Theseus myth, the same strategy should prove even more helpful in the House of Pride episode where Spenser provides two direct references: Theseus's damnation "to endlesse slouth by law," and the story of Hippolytus. The latter need not detain us, since Judith H. Anderson has noted the essential points. "The story of Hippolytus," she writes, "comments on Redcrosse's condition only by being itself." Anderson argues that it is a psychomachia in which Redcrosse plays all the key roles: faithless and lustful, like Phaedra, in his abandonment of Una and in his dalliance with Duessa; "too simply chaste," like Hippolytus, which I take to mean naively virginal; and too quick to judge, like the "raging, wrathful Theseus."[30] I would add only that in Spenser's version of the story Phaedra's suicide with a knife directly anticipates Redcrosse's near suicide with the dagger that Despaire gives him (v.39, ix.51). Phaedra's knife is unique to Spenser,[31] directly anticipates the knight's own nadir and exemplifies the end that he narrowly escapes. Before considering Theseus's damnation, we need to note how the House of Pride parodies the Cretan labyrinth and introduces another episode in the Theseus myth, his descent into hell.

A reading of the House of Pride in terms of the Cretan labyrinth rests partly on an architectural parallel between the two structures. The original Cretan labyrinth may have been the palace of Minos at Knossos, with a dungeon beneath: "The notion as to the Labyrinth having been a prison from which escape was impossible may also have some connection with two deep pits beneath the palace, whose function was possibly that of dungeons for prisoners."[32] Of course, modern archeology does not directly illuminate *The Faerie Queene*. Rather the point is that palace-dungeon-cave-labyrinth, a powerful nexus in the human imagination, is as relevant to Spenser's treatment of the underworld as to ancient architecture. As a palace that provides easy access but whose dungeon makes escape difficult, the Cretan labyrinth corresponds to Spenser's description of the House of Pride:

> Great troupes of people traueild thitherward
> Both day and night, of each degree and place,
> But few returned, hauing scaped hard,
> With balefull beggerie, or foule disgrace,
> Which euer after in most wretched case,
> Like loathsome lazars, by the hedges lay. (iv.3)

And inside, the dwarf "had spide, / Where in a dongeon deepe huge numbers lay / Of caytiue wretched thrals, that wayled night and day" (v.45). People who enter the House of Pride experience—or have already experienced—a moral version of a walker's disorientation in a labyrinth.[33] Of course, the knight's disorientation is moral as well as psychological, for the House of Pride is an example of labyrinths of sin "woven by the maze-walker himself, either directly or because he has rendered himself prey to Satan of his own free will."[34] As a breakdown of correct perception and a loss of touch with one's goals, the labyrinth nicely characterizes the Redcrosse knight's abandonment of his quest and his embrace of the wrong values embodied by Duessa, Lucifera, and Satan himself.

While the House of Pride, both as a type of physical threat and as the occasion of mental confusion, resembles the palace of Knossos, the episode offers a parody of Ariadne's thread. The thread now represents perverted human sympathy—sensual love as opposed to spiritual love—which focuses on Duessa and leads *into* the labyrinth. Duessa parodies Una's "Add faith vnto your force" when she calls out, "Thine the shield, and I, and all" (v.11). Although the remark may be addressed to either Redcrosse or Sans Joy (she is covering her bases), Redcrosse responds with "quickning faith" (12)—whether in God or Duessa or himself the reader is not sure—which recalls his equally ambiguous "more then manly force" (i.14). After he wins the battle, he still needs the thread of grace made active by faith but receives instead the dwarf's description of Lucifera's dungeon. The dwarf himself ought to be a reminder of the proper human sympathy that Una represents, but it is more the cowardly desire to avoid a negative (imprisonment) than the genuine inclination to affirm a positive (Una, his quest) that motivates the knight to leave. Contrary to the notion that "dwarfism" is associated with "the subordination of reason,"[35] the role of Una's dwarf in the House of Pride episode suggests reason's ability to reassert itself and save an individual from destruction. If the dwarf's account merely activates the knight's right reason and momentarily restores his sense of direction, the episode reveals Redcrosse's deficiency: Theseus, the natural man holding the ball of thread, is more in touch with normal human sympathy than the knight of holiness.

Given the strong connection in the *Aeneid* between labyrinth and underworld, the House of Pride is also a kind of hell. The myth of the Cretan labyrinth foreshadows Theseus's descent into hell, and the latter is a variation on the earlier motif. The "forest and the tangled dens / of beasts" at Cumae are maze-like, and Aeneas passes through gates on which Daedalus has carved the Cretan labyrinth (VI.10-11, 38-43).[36] The motif of the labyrinth continues with a description of the setting in which Aeneas searches for the Sibyl and perhaps also with her own labyrinthine words (60-64). According to modern archeology "the Sibyl's cave lies at the end of a long man-made tunnel with lateral galleries and rooms branching off, and finally three rooms of which the last is further subdivided into three. The place itself, like Virgil's description, is quite labyrinthine."[37] Maze and underworld are even more closely related because a maze indicates "a change of state, from one kind of life to another."[38] The juxtaposition suggests the kind of transition that Aeneas is about to undergo, a death to his Trojan past and a rebirth to his Roman destiny.[39] For Virgil, then, the labyrinth is a prefiguration and emblem of the underworld, which is a kind of labyrinth itself insofar as it is easy to enter but hard to escape:

> . . . easy—
> the way that leads into Avernus: day
> and night the door of darkest Dis is open.
> But to recall your steps, to rise again
> into the upper air: that is the labor;
> that is the task. (VI.175-80)

Connections between labyrinth and underworld suggest that the Cretan labyrinth foreshadows the hell in which Theseus is confined. There is a similar relationship between the labyrinthine wood of Errour and the House of Pride: once entered, error can lead to the deadly sins personified at the House of Pride, which are a moral hell.

Theseus's own descent into hell and capture by Pluto illuminate the episode at the House of Pride, which offers parody in return and foreshadows the knight's imprisonment in Orgoglio's dungeon. Here is the tale. Theseus and Pirithous, both widowers, decided to wed daughters of Zeus. They drew lots for Helen, Theseus won, but because she was only ten years old she was sent to live with his mother. Pirithous wanted Persephone. When they demanded her from Pluto, they were told to be seated in what turned out to be Chairs of Forgetfulness, which immediately became part of their bodies.[40] Four years later, Hercules, in hell to capture Cerberus, helped Theseus escape, but Pirithous could not be saved. By this time Helen was gone and had made Theseus's mother her slave.[41]

Theseus's entrance into hell without a golden bough as tribute and his attempt to carry off Persephone are acts of pride analogous to the Redcrosse knight's own prideful abandonment of his quest and his insistence on pursuing the wrong path. Both suffer forgetfulness or a loss of direction: Theseus, so that he forgets knowledge of the gods that he should not possess; Redcrosse, as a mark of his error. Consequently, neither is a successful harrower of hell. As Theseus fails to get Persephone for Pirithous or to save his friend, Redcrosse leaves the House of Pride without liberating any of those held captive in Lucifera's dungeon. Moreover, both Theseus and Redcrosse require the assistance of another— Hercules and the dwarf, respectively. In this detail, the House of Pride anticipates the fulfillment of the parallel to the Theseus story in the knight's rescue from Orgoglio's dungeon by Arthur, the true Hercules- or Christ-figure. (Spenser is borrowing details from the harrowing of hell story in this episode and elsewhere in Book I; these matters are discussed in Chapter Three.) That the dungeon represents hell is evident because Redcrosse suffers the same denial of hope and movement that Theseus experiences in *Aeneid* VI.

5. Justice and Damnation

Unlike Theseus in the myth of the Chair of Forgetfulness, Virgil's Theseus may actually be in full possession of his wits. In John W. Zarker's reading of *Aeneid* VI, it is Theseus who "warns all the Phlegyae (Phlegyas, Ixion, Pirithous, and the Lapiths) that, [fore]warned by his example, they should learn justice, i.e. proper conduct toward their fellow men, and respect for the gods."[42] Like Redcrosse at the cave of Despaire, Theseus is painfully aware of his past sins, and memory becomes an aspect of damnation. Since Theseus in classical myth is condemned for pride to sloth, the nature of his damnation is a quality that opposes his essential self.[43] A man who virtually founds a city, slays the Minotaur, seeks the fleece, and so on, is vital in a way that would make sloth, coupled with a keen awareness of his sins and the impossibility of release or even movement, the severest possible punishment. His is not a Dantesque damnation, in which the punishment is of the same nature as the crime; it is a state opposite the hero's most basic virtues. So it is with Redcrosse, whose faith reaches a nadir in Canto 9 when he has a bitter taste of hell pain at the cave of Despaire before being drawn back to faith by Una, the Ariadne-figure, who reminds him of mercy (ix.53). As noted in Chapter One, grace is the thread of escape from suicidal despair, much as it enables a return from a literal underworld, as in Spenser's echo of the *Aeneid* just prior to Duessa's descent with Sansjoy (v.31).

Being condemned "by law" puts Theseus in the same position as Aesculapius, whose punishment is eternal in Spenser but not in classical literature. The physician's "endlesse" damnation in stanza 42 matches that of Theseus,[44] so that in *The Faerie Queene* both represent the negative end of natural man. On the positive side, Plutarch comments on Theseus's natural and moral excellence: "He was comen to the prime and lustines of his youth, and . . . with the strength of his bodie he shewed a great courage, joyned with a naturall wisedome, and stayednes of wit."[45] Unredeemed, however, Theseus ironically becomes like those Plutarch immediately goes on to describe, squandering his natural endowments on actions unbecoming an ideal Athenian citizen.

> For the worlde at that time brought forth men, which for strongnesse in their armes, for swyftnes of feete, and for a generall strength of the whole bodye, dyd farre passe the common force of others, and were never wearie for any labour or travell they tooke in hande. But for all this, they never employed these giftes of nature to any honest or profitable thing, but rather delighted villanously to hurte and wronge others: as if all the fruite and profit of their extraordinary strength had consisted in crueltye, and violence only, and to be able to keepe others under and in subjection, and to force, destroye, and spoyle all that came to their handes.[46]

Theseus declines from the virtue of youthful prowess and good deeds toward vice and other wrongdoing in later life—a falling motion exactly opposite that of Redcrosse, whose youthful error yields to mature holiness. As a result, their ultimate fates also contrast: damnation for pride to endlesse sloth versus sainthood and eternal life in the Heavenly Jerusalem. Since Theseus's natural excellence is not supported by grace or even proper behavior like that of those who will dwell in Elysium, damnation results from the same strict justice that he dispenses early in his career.

> And going a litle further, he slewe Damastes, otherwise surnamed Procrustes, in the cittie of Hermionia: and that by stretching him out, to make him even with the length and measure of his beddes, as he was wont to doe unto straungers that passed by. Theseus dyd that after the imitation of Hercules, who punished tyrannes with the selfe same payne and torment, which they had made others suffer. . . . Thus proceeded Theseus after this selfe manner, punishing the wicked in like sorte, justly compelling them tabyde the same payne and torments, which they before had unjustly made others abyde.[47]

Theseus's action against assorted villains embodies a Dantesque version of punishment: the penalty, which captures the essential nature of the crime, is much like the penalty Minos, who later becomes judge in hell, imposes on Athens for the death of his son. Although Theseus in hell suffers the *inverse* of his sometimes-criminal vitality in life, he represents, as both avenger and prisoner, the rigid law Despaire proposes to Redcrosse, which is the final word outside the realm of grace and the opposite of Christian mercy: "The greater sin, the greater punishment" (ix.43).[48]

Indifferent to or unaware of rewards and punishments in the afterlife, Theseus indulges in brutality and lust. Since he ignores the fact that life is a multicursal journey in search of an exit to another plane of existence, his moral wandering reflects the labyrinthine world in which he lives. Put another way, he lacks what Redcrosse receives at the House of Holiness—a vision of the New Jerusalem and the awareness that he will become Saint George (x.55ff.). The labyrinth again provides the right metaphor: Theseus and Redcrosse are both "maze treaders," but at the House of Holiness Redcrosse becomes a "maze viewer" as well.[49] Theseus and Redcrosse, like Redcrosse and his former self, have contrasting perspectives on the labyrinth that is life. Viewed from within, the labyrinth is "a bewildering process, a dynamic prison"; viewed from above, it is "a static artifact, a magnificent product of human ingenuity,"[50] or, for Redcrosse, of divine providence. The knight achieves through Christian vision a transcendent view of material reality, a perspective similar to that of Daedalus, who, when imprisoned in the labyrinth for giving Ariadne the ball of thread, makes wings to escape.[51] In short, the Christian faith is the only way to transcend a world-bound view of human life. Although Redcrosse cannot see the turns in the road through the labyrinth, he can choose paths leading in the general direction of his ultimate destination. Thus an individual Christian life has the same purposeful shape as sacred history, in contrast to the bleak classical view in which Theseus degenerates and is finally murdered.

It does not follow, however, that "having subdued the flesh, he [Redcrosse] can leave the labyrinth for freedom to achieve his destiny as Saint George."[52] If Redcrosse had left the labyrinth of sensuality, there would be no letter from Duessa in Canto 12. A successful journey is a matter of proper orientation within and toward the labyrinth, not of escape from it. Equally certainly, his life will end positively, for the following reason:

> There is also a labyrinth with a happy ending, a metaphorical labyrinth-as-process, carefully shaped by a master architect to direct the worthy wanderer to a profitable end: the path, the choices between paths, the prescribed *errores*, all are designed to carry the wanderer over just the right territory to achieve something that could not have been reached by a direct route. The architect knows that a certain process is necessary if the wanderer is to get where the architect wants him to go and learn what should be learned.[53]

This statement sums up what is also true of the Redcrosse knight: wisdom and spiritual maturity must be earned on the road through error and cannot be gained on a more direct path. The labyrinth is a permanent and necessary condition of life, which the Protestant knight must negotiate alone, with faith providing the Daedalus-dimension. As a reading of Book I must be "Not without Theseus," so must it also be not without grace, faith's response to which enables the knight to move beyond the slaying of outer foes (where Theseus stops) to the refinement of character and spirit that Redcrosse achieves.

6. Spenser's Use of Myth

The foregoing analysis of the Redcrosse knight in light of the Theseus myth is consistent with Spenser's use of classical myth throughout Book I: myth provides a negative gloss on Spenser's Christian myth of the individual, and their juxtaposition highlights the shortcomings of Redcrosse, the archetypal Protestant knight.[54] Theseus is a fine example of this principle—a Redcrosse who never leaves the House of Pride, a clear emblem of the knight's early faults, and a warning of the damnation he risks. To the extent that Redcrosse moves beyond an early identification with Theseus, however, Spenser's use of the myth is ultimately much like Virgil's. In both the *Aeneid* and *The Faerie Queene* Theseus contrasts with the hero. As Aeneas will achieve greater piety than Theseus, Redcrosse transcends both classical figures in his journey to holiness. The knight will live forever as St. George in the Heavenly Jerusalem, Aeneas will only dwell in Elysium, and the fate of Theseus is utter damnation.

CHAPTER THREE
PRINCE ARTHUR AND CHRIST'S DESCENT INTO HELL IN BOOKS I AND II

As noted in Chapter Two, Theseus carries two things with him into the Cretan labyrinth: a ball of string, which helps him find his way out after slaying the Minotaur, and a ball of pitch, which he jams into the monster's mouth to prevent it from biting him. In the Middle Ages, the story of Theseus in the labyrinth was allegorized as Christ's descent into hell, with the thread as His divine nature and the pitch as His human nature.[1] Christ descended into hell not merely in His Godhead or in His human soul but in a dynamic unity of both.

In *Mirrors of Celestial Grace*, his 1994 study of patristic theology in *The Faerie Queene*, Harold L. Weatherby takes a position in harmony with the above point and against that of such critics as A. S. P. Woodhouse and Patrick Cullen, who regard Book I as the realm of grace and Book II as the realm of nature. Weatherby offers the following summary of Cullen's argument. In Mammon's cave Guyon "makes a 'Christlike assertion of virtue' which he cannot live up to; the abortive attempt 'reveals the Adamic limits of [his] virtue.' . . . Guyon tries to defeat the devil—to play Christ—without access to that grace by means of a 'classical or purely human temperance' which 'can hold the devil at bay, though' . . . not vanquish him as Christ did. The faint is the 'inevitable culmination of the Adamic weakness he has manifested throughout the ordeal.'" Cullen's solution "is to separate Christ's humanity from His divinity. Guyon becomes Christ and thus fulfills the expectations of Spenser's symbolism by an 'approximation' to Christ *as man* but not to Christ as God. That means that Guyon imitates Christ adequately in the wilderness but not in the Harrowing." Because "Christ performed the

Harrowing divinely, Guyon, without grace, cannot be Christ in that venture."
Weatherby points out, however, that Spenser

> would have been unlikely to isolate Christ's humanity from His
> divinity or to have suggested that in one of the great soteriological
> mysteries Christ acted only as man and in another as both God and
> man. The second of the thirty-nine Articles says explicitly and
> firmly that the 'two whole and perfect Natures . . . were joined
> together in one Person, *never to be divided*' (italics added [by
> Weatherby]). . . . There can obviously, therefore, be no such thing
> as an *imitatio Christi* which pertains only to the Lord's humanity,
> for in the Incarnation not only is God man but Man is God.

Weatherby's conclusion is that Guyon's descent and subsequent faint are in
harmony with the notion of this unified dual nature. Far from saying that the faint
indicates natural virtue operating without the aid of grace, he sees Guyon as
microchristus because of the faint: "To win the victory over Satan (or Mammon)
through Christ's all-powerful divinity, man must conform himself to the weakness
of Christ's humanity."[2] In this way, Weatherby challenges the generally accepted
distinction between Book I as the realm of grace and Book II as the realm of
nature.

What Weatherby does not discuss in sufficient detail is the role of Arthur
as a Christ-figure in parallel passages. In Book I, Canto 8, Arthur rescues
Redcrosse from Orgoglio's dungeon, an action that recalls Christ's leading
righteous souls out of hell; in Book II, Canto 8, Arthur defends the unconscious
Guyon by killing Cymochles and Pyrochles. Arthur's role in these episodes
upholds rather than contradicts the distinction between nature and grace that
Weatherby challenges. After all, as Anthea Hume points out, Guyon's faith
(II.i.27) means that he cannot be a natural man.[3] I prefer, however, to qualify both
Cullen and Weatherby and to propose a new middle view. If Books I and II are
not a dichotomy of grace and nature but a continuum of different types of grace,
then there can be an *imitatio Christi* that pertains only to Christ's humanity, and
Guyon in Mammon's cave imitates Christ in the harrowing of hell.

In one sense, there is no such thing as a realm of nature because grace is *part* of the virtues we consider to be natural. Although lacking the actual grace found in Book I (this type of grace is bestowed for the performance of specific actions and may exist even in the unbaptized),[4] Book II is nevertheless a realm in which common grace is active. Calvin dislikes the notion that human beings by nature seek after the good, but he does acknowledge that the good in us, which God bestows, is corrupted but not destroyed by the Fall. This natural endowment—common grace or "the light of nature"—centers on reason.[5] So Books I and II, which appear to Woodhouse and Cullen as two realms, one of grace and another of nature, are really a continuum of grace, different in their degree of direct assistance. When we say that Book II is the realm of nature, we really mean that it is the realm of common grace.

Along with acknowledging my presupposition, I should address Weatherby's, which is simply that the works of the Church Fathers—e.g., John Chrysostom, Cyril of Jerusalem, Dionysius the Areopagite, and Ambrose— "account for the way [Spenser] represents . . . the Harrowing of Hell."[6] To apply Christ's harrowing of hell to *The Faerie Queene* on the basis of the Church Fathers alone, however, is to overlook material more to Spenser's historical context. It is true that the Thirty-Nine Articles affirm the unity of Christ, but it is equally true that in the 1500s there was a controversy centering on the statement in the Apostles' Creed, "He descended into hell."

1. Christ's Descent into Hell

However "explicitly and firmly" Article Two affirms that Christ's two natures, once joined, were indivisible, there appears to be a debate in Spenser's age on this issue. In reference to the Creed, sixteenth-century commentators diligently analyzed every aspect of Christ's descent and disagreed not only about whether Christ descended into a local hell but also about the manner of his going there.[7] How, they wondered, could Christ liberate the Old Testament righteous from hell and be with the thief in paradise at the same time? While most held that he came as a conqueror, it is unclear whether he visited hell in his human nature or in a unity of his human and divine natures.

The first possibility is that Christ's body, soul and Godhead could be in separate locations. As Adam Hill writes, "He was in the Sepulchre according to his body, and in hell according to his soull; but as God he was both in Paradise and with the theefe, and in the throne with the Father and the Holy Ghost."[8] Thomas Becon, too, holds that Christ descended to hell in his soul:

> Christ, after the death of his body, went down in his soul to hell, as clearly appeareth by the scriptures; not that he should there suffer more pains (which he had already on the cross suffered to the uttermost, and done whatsoever was needful for our redemption), but to break the pride of Satan, and to destroy the fury of hellish powers against the chosen people of god, that all the faithful thereby might be delivered from death and hell, and triumphantly say with the prophet: "O death, I will be thy death; O hell, I will be thy destruction."[9]

This passage depicts Christ in hell as a conqueror, and he becomes all the more glorious for triumphing as a man. Indeed, his victory would seem pointless to Becon if he had triumphed in his Godhead alone. Whereas it would take very little for God to overthrow hell, the same action requires a great deal from a human soul and thus signifies the way in which an individual person, with Christ's assistance, can overcome the powers of hell on a personal level.

A second view asserts the unity of Christ's soul and Godhead in hell. As in Henry VIII's "Institution of a Christian Man," Christ "descended immediately in his soul down into hell, leaving his most blessed body here in earth, and . . . at his coming thither, by the incomparable might and force of his godhead, he entered into hell."[10] Similarly, John Longland affirms the unity of Christ's humanity and divinity in his Good Friday sermon: "These thre dayes whiles this bodye laye deade in the sepulchre, the soul of Christe Joyned to his godhede, descended to the helles."[11]

Despite Article Two's insistance on Christs unity, there appears to have been some disagreement about the divine and human nature of Christ in the descent. If it is fair for Weatherby to argue that Spenser was exposed to the writings of the Church Fathers at Pembroke, then I think that it is fair to assume that he may have been aware of the range of possible interpretations of the Creed in his own century. Accordingly, Arthur calls to mind not only a unity of Christ's divinity and humanity in Book I, Canto 8, but also his human soul alone in Book II, Canto 8.

2. Prince Arthur in Parallel Passages

The link between Christ and Prince Arthur is strengthened by numerous sources that describe Christ in his descent as a knight or prince. In the Gospel of Nicodemus he is a "princely fighter," the "Lord strong and mighty, the Lord mighty in battle." In *Piers the Ploughman* he is "the image of a prince," "a young knight preparing himself for a battle with the Devil," and "a prince, who finally wins the victory over Death and becomes a king and conqueror through His prowess"; in short, "Christ is the Christians' conqueror." In Passus 18, for example, Langland writes, "A man came riding along barefoot on an ass, unarmed without spurs. He looked like the good Samaritan—or was it Piers the Ploughman? He was young and lusty, like a squire coming to be dubbed knight and receive his golden spurs and cut-away shoes." The editor notes that buckling on spurs was an essential part of the ceremony of dubbing a knight. "Cut-away shoes" refers to the fashion of slitting or slashing them by way of ornament. In a similar way, the Old English poem "The Harrowing of Hell" calls Christ "the Prince of all peoples," king, Lord of hosts, and peerless majesty. Becon says that Christ descended "as a valiant prince, and as a most puissant and glorious king." Calvin, too, refers to Christ as "our Prince," perhaps an echo of the "Prince of

54

Peace" (Isaiah 9:6).[12]

Finding in Arthur the distinction between Christ's divinity and humanity is in line with the critical consensus, and a close examination of the two episodes bears out the distinction I would make between Books I and II. First, Book I, Canto 8, calls to mind the notion of Christ harrowing hell in a unity of his divinity and humanity. Spenser calls attention to Arthur's mortality in the description of Orgoglio's blows: "The stroke vpon his shield so heauie lites, / That to the ground it doubleth him full low: / What mortall wight could euer beare so monstrous blow?" (18). While bent low in a show of mortal vulnerability, Arthur is unhurt because of his diamond shield, which at this point is just a shield with superior protective qualities. So far, Arthur is using his natural physical endowments to fight the personification of spiritual pride. But the only way to win a battle against the idea that you do not need grace is *by grace*, which erupts the instant the shield is uncovered. Orgoglio, the Satan-figure, is immediately blinded and rendered helpless now that Arthur, the Christ-like rescuer, is aided by the shield's incredible light, which symbolizes the power of the Godhead and recalls the way Christ brought light to the dark reaches of hell. As Spenser puts it, "As where th'Almighties lightning brond does light, / It dimmes the dazed eyen, and daunts the senses quight" (21). Woodhouse calls this "the violence of grace."[13] The Christian God has become a kind of Jove, bestowing actual grace—the grace often experienced as God-given strength—at a key moment in the battle.

Anthea Hume rightly observes that "the divine power which is ready to intervene on man's behalf . . . does not mean that Arthur . . . *becomes* Christ during the canto" (my emphasis).[14] But that Arthur, who represents the virtue to which a particular book is devoted (in this case, holiness), should be Christ's imitator—a Christ *figure*—is consistent with Jesus's statement in John 14:12: "Verely, verely I say vnto you, he that beleueth in me, the workes that I do, he shall do also, & greater then these shal he do: for I go vnto my Father." Christ's role as a rescuer is clearly expressed in Psalm 68:18: "Thou art gone vp on high:

thou hast led captiuitie captiue, and receiued giftes for men: yea, euen the rebellious hast thou led, that the Lord God might dwell there." Similarly, the Redcrosse knight's defeat of the half-dragon Errour, his defeat in Canto 11 of the dragon, and his liberation of Adam and Eve from the brazen tower also borrow details from the harrowing of hell story. For example, the brazen tower relates to the gates of hell: "For he hathe broken the gates of brasse, and brast the barres of yron a sundre" (Psalm 107:16).[15]

Whereas Arthur's battle in Book I, Canto 8, reflects Christ's dual nature in the harrowing of hell, Book II, Canto 8, in ways harmonious with the (for Weatherby defunct) notion of the realm of nature, presents Arthur fighting, as before, using the strength of his physical attributes but this time without the supernatural assistance of his shield. Fighting in the power of his natural virtue suggests common grace unaided by the actual grace that helps him in his earlier battle. Now the diamond shield is covered (17), and his sword, which is also supernatural, does not aid him because Pyrochles wields it. Hard pressed, Arthur is eventually wounded in the side, much as Christ was wounded in the side on the cross. The latter wound clearly suggests the distinction between Christ's human nature and his Godhead: during the crucifixion the Godhead does not intervene to spare the mortal body from pain and suffering; nor does actual grace help Arthur in his efforts to defend the sleeping Guyon. When Arthur finally kills Cymochles and then Pyrochles, he does so with *Guyon's* sword, which the Palmer gives him and which represents reason. Whereas supernatural assistance is needed to overcome a spiritual foe like Orgoglio, psychological foes (Pyrochles, wrath; Cymochles, the human penchant for luxury) are battled by reason, which is God-given to be sure but is also a natural part of the human condition.[16]

3. Psychomachia

Books I and II thus present different versions of the psychomachia.[17] In Book I, the human soul is imprisoned in the face of total depravity. Actual grace, an external force personified by Arthur, helps liberate Redcrosse from spiritual pride and from the damnation to which it leads. As a result, the knight achieves a proper orientation toward God and his own soul. In Book II, common grace or God-given human resources help Guyon overcome merely psychological problems and achieve a proper orientation toward his own psyche. Here grace exists on the human plane, as Guyon suggests when he thanks Arthur for his "most gratious ayd" and for the "so great graces" he has shown (viii.55). Indeed Arthur's reply is followed by this statement: "So goodly purpose they together fond, / Of kindnesse and of curteous aggrace" (56). So it is not that Book I is the realm of grace and Book II the realm of nature. More accurately, Spenser explores types of grace that are appropriate to the books' respective virtues, and Arthur's parallel battles have an analogue in the sixteenth-century debate on the manner of Christ's descending into hell: divine and human against Orgoglio, merely human against Pyrochles and Cymochles.

If Weatherby's premise about the unity of Christ's divine and human nature in the descent into hell admits exception, then so may his conclusion that Guyon's descent and the faint it causes are part of an analogue to Christ's unified nature and an essential part of his role as *microchristus*.[18] I would argue that Guyon, in terms of descent, can be *microchristus* in Mammon's cave with or without an analogue that unifies divinity and humanity.

Using patristic tradition, Weatherby argues convincingly that Guyon may not be guilty of the sin of curiosity when he decides to descend into Mammon's cave; indeed, if he showed any interest in its contents, he would be destroyed, as Mammon threatens. (In Chapter Four, using a New Historical approach, I suggest that curiosity seems likely in other episodes.) But descent in the 1590 *Faerie Queene*, whether it be to a hell, a cave, or merely a symbolic underworld like the House of Pride, repeatedly involves a confrontation with personal weakness and the potential for sinfulness. Redcrosse falls into concupiscence, pride, and despair before he is saved by grace; Britomart encounters her own potential for solipsistic fantasy in Merlin's cave and, like Arthur, is nicked by Busirane before she binds him and frees Amoret; and when Guyon faints, revealing the body's limits, he necessarily undergoes the transformation from classical temperance based on a person's fortitude to Christian temperance, which is open to outside assistance and marked by the angel's pledge of future protection. In this respect, my reading of *The Faerie Queene* is reactionary, for it affirms Cullen's earlier view.

Guyon's experience is thus consistent with what Calvin says each individual must undergo:

> Let even the most perfect man descend into his own conscience and call his deeds to account, what then will be the outcome for him? Will he sweetly rest as if all things were well composed between him and God and not, rather, be torn by dire torments, since if he be judged by works, he will feel grounds for condemnation within himself? The conscience, if it looks to God, must either have sure peace with his judgment or be beseiged by the terrors of hell.[19]

In terms of content, Calvin's statement seems more appropriate to a description of the Redcrosse knight's multiple errors in Book I than to the Knight of Temperance who really does not do anything wrong. But *structurally*, Calvin's description of an individual's encounter with what must be overcome pertains as much to Guyon as to Redcrosse. As Christ descends not just into the underworld but also into hell-like despair on the cross to achieve humanity's salvation, each person descends into his or her own soul in order to confront what must be overcome. By resisting Mammon without the supernatural assistance Arthur receives in his battle with Orgoglio, Guyon reaches his physical limits and faints. It is this temperance, based on physical and psychological capacity unsupported by a higher-than-common grace, that he must transcend.

Weatherby is right to ask how "can a genuine *microchristus* do other than faint,"[20] but Guyon does not win a victory over Mammon "through Christ's all-powerful divinity." The *disunity*-in-descent of Christ's two natures suggests not only that Guyon's experience in Mammon's cave parallels Christ's harrowing (and not merely His temptation in the wilderness) but also that Guyon resists temptation underground in a way that is harmonious with a qualified nature-and-grace approach.

CHAPTER FOUR

THE CRIMINAL UNDERWORLD
AND GUYON'S CONTINENCE IN BOOK II

A resemblance between Redcrosse and the Knight of Temperance not mentioned in A. C. Hamilton's study of the parallels[1] is their similar premarital situations. Redcrosse, young and inexperienced, is betrothed to Una only at the end of Book I, and as René Graziani notes, "Spenser may have envisaged Guyon as relatively young—Elyot thought seventeen was the age a young man was ready for the *Nicomachean Ethics.*"[2] In one sense Guyon apparently begins where Redcrosse ends up, for as he tells Mammon in response to the offer of marriage to Philotime: "Yet is my trouth yplight, / And loue auowd to other Lady late, / That to remoue the same I have no might" (vii.50). As these details suggest, both Redcrosse and Guyon must make a perilous transition from adolescent to adult sexuality by achieving the balance of desire and restraint that temporarily eludes the young lovers in *A Midsummer Night's Dream.* Benjamin G. Lockerd, Jr., expresses this basic idea: "Guyon's quest, then, deals not with how love must be approached in general but with how it must be taken at this moment of blossoming into adolescence."[3] The knight, however, is blossoming not into but out of adolescence, with lust being one of the great dangers to temperance and holiness that both he and Redcrosse must face. By succumbing to looseness, Redcrosse commits spiritual and carnal fornication with the whore Duessa (I.vii.7), who, as Douglas Waters demonstrates, represents the whore of Babylon and the Roman Catholic Church.[4] That Redcrosse will still marry Una despite his errors indicates not only the fact that one who falls can be redeemed by grace but also a double standard that obtained in the Renaissance: Una must remain a

"*Faire virgin*" (Canto 8, headnote), but Redcrosse is sexually initiated not without consequences but with eventual impunity by a whore.

In Book II Phaedria and Acrasia attempt a similar seduction of Guyon, but since *The Faerie Queene* is historical allegory the question is whether these temptresses have analogues parallel to the role of the Roman Catholic Church in Book I. If Duessa represents spiritual prostitution, the analogy in the realm of moral virtue may be the actual physical act of prostitution, which prospered in the century framing Spenser's poem. E. J. Burford states that a population explosion and economic difficulties between 1550 and 1650 generated a plenteous yet tellingly insufficient supply of women for brothels, street prostitution, and mistress relationships, and he quotes *Platten's Travels in 1599* as stating that "'although close watch is kept on them [the whores] swarms of these women haunt the town [of London] in the taverns and playhouses.'"[5] Prostitution was an "endemic feature of London life during the sixteenth and seventeenth centuries,"[6] for, as the Bridewell records show, at least one hundred brothels were operating in the late 1570s.[7]

Attitudes toward prostitution were polarized. Some writers stressed what Charles Bernheimer calls "the physical reality of degraded female sexuality"[8] and "paint[ed] the prostitute as 'the prey of the bawd and debauchee', a figure of misery and pity, 'unprotected', 'unwary', 'ruined' and 'enslaved.'"[9] Others associated "female sexuality with filth and disease," especially after the appearance of syphilis in the 1490s,[10] and regarded the whore as "the temptress who enticed and then trapped men in her lascivious net; she was the agent of unbridled lust."[11] Even religious leaders who, like Hugh Latimer, called attention to the plight of the poor showed no compassion toward prostitutes.[12] Spenser's treatment of Phaedria and Acrasia echoes the latter misogynistic attitude, for his intention is not to allegorize the degradation of women but to examine a man's psychological responses to lust. Nonetheless, since Spenser could not have been unaware of the underworld of 1580s London, prostitution provides a relevant and long-overlooked analogy for the Legend of Temperance. By using Renaissance prostitution to contextualize temperance and continence in the Idle Lake and Bower of Bliss episodes, this chapter asserts, contrary to the critical consensus, that Guyon's continence overshadows his temperance.

1. Coryate Meets a Courtesan

Thomas Coryate, who toured western Europe for fifteen months, arrived in Venice on June 21, 1608, eighteen years after Spenser published the first three books of *The Faerie Queene*.[13] Although it cannot be argued that the resulting travel book *Coryat's Crudities* influenced anything in Book II, it seems likely that an English gentleman like Coryate would have known the poem and possible that he may have seen himself as a seventeenth-century Guyon. Certainly his attitudes toward Venice participated in the same cultural stereotypes that had existed nearly a generation earlier. In the 1590s "the self-image of Venice as a maiden or virgin city" (and thus linked to Queen Elizabeth) contrasted with an opposite view of the city as the scarlet woman (Venice and Venus being frequent puns).[14] The dual nature of Fidessa/Duessa is relevant here because her virginity, a mere appearance (I.ii.24, II.i.21), parallels the way Venice's legendary courtesans overshadowed (at least in the mind of Coryate) the portrayal of Venice as a virgin.

It is not my purpose to argue for Spenser's influence on Coryate. The two texts differ radically: whereas Coryate describes a visit to a specific courtesan and gives general information about Venetian whores and their business, Spenser's allegory provides what Aristotle calls the "universal event" whose purpose is not to portray historical specifics but to examine what it is like for a man to lose or maintain his hold on temperance in the face of the sort of sensual temptation brothels embody.[15] My purpose is rather to show, through numerous parallels, that Guyon's sojourn with Phaedria on Idle Lake is sufficiently similar to Coryate's visit to the courtesan Margarita Æmeliana that unpacking the tourist's psychology may illuminate the knight's.

Indeed, Book II and Coryate's section on Venetian courtesans have some striking similarities. Spenser's description of Idle Lake—"this wide Inland sea" (vi.10)—is "probably a literal translation of *Mediterranean*. Along with the 'gondelay' . . . [vi.2] of Phaedria, the name helps to evoke an association between Italy and a life of idle pleasure."[16] And the imagery of the Bower of Bliss, especially the arbors and water fountains, links Canto 12 with Italy.[17] These details strengthen the parallels between Phaedria and Acrasia, and between the two temptresses and the realm of Coryate's travels. Moreover, like Guyon, who encounters five siren-like mermaids (one for each physical sense) on his boat journey to the island of Acrasia, the Circe-figure, Coryate's encounter with the courtesan is self-consciously Homeric:

> Also the ornaments of her body are so rich, that except thou dost even geld thy affections (a thing hardly to be done) or carry with thee Ulysses hearbe called Moly which is mentioned by Homer, that is, some antidote against these Venereous titillations, she wil very neare benumme and captivate thy senses. . . .

> Moreover shee will endeavour to enchaunt thee partly with her melodious notes that she warbles upon her lute, which she fingers with as laudable a stroake as many men that are excellent professors in the noble science of Musicke; and partly with that heart-tempting harmony of her voice.

> I will give thee the same counsell that Lipsius did to a friend of his that was to travell into Italy, even to furnish thy selfe with a double armour, the one for thine eyes, the other for thine eares. As for thine eyes, shut them and turne them aside from these venereous Venetian objects. For they are the double windowes that conveigh them to thy heart. Also thou must fortifie thine eares against the attractive inchauntments of their plausible speeches.[18]

Here is Coryate, the nouveau Ulysses who has encountered Circe and the Sirens, conveying moly in the form of good advice to his readers who may one day travel to Italy—they must stop up their ears and eyes so that the courtesans do not infect their imaginations (the thing that his titillating text, of course, simultaneously does).

Coryate introduces his section on courtesans as follows:

> But since I have taken occasion to mention some notable
> particulars of their women, I will insist farther upon that matter,
> and make relation of their Cortezans also, as being a thing incident
> and very proper to this discourse, especially because the name of a
> Cortezan of Venice is famoused all over Christendome. And I
> have here inserted a picture of one of their nobler Cortezans,
> according to her Venetian habites, with my owne neare unto her,
> made in that forme as we saluted each other. Surely by so much
> the more willing I am to treat something of them, because I
> perceive it is so rare a matter to find a description of Venetian
> Cortezans in any Author, that all the writers that I could ever see,
> which have described the city, have altogether excluded them out
> of their writings. Therefore seeing the History of these famous
> gallants is omitted by all others that have written just
> Commentaries of the Venetian state, as I know it is not impertinent
> to this present Discourse to write of them; so I hope it will not be
> which no Author whatsoever doth impart unto him but my selfe.
> Onely I feare least I shall expose my selfe to the severe censure and
> scandalous imputations of many carping Criticks, who I thinke will
> tax me for luxury and wantonnesse to insert so lascivious a matter
> into this Treatise of Venice. Wherefore at the end of this discourse
> of the Cortezans I will in some sort satisfie them, if they are not too
> captious.[19]

Coryate incorrectly claims to be the first to write about courtesans—William
Thomas, who had visited Venice seventy years earlier, devotes a paragraph to
them[20]—but he may well be the first to write an extended piece on the topic. After
discussing the etymology of "Cortezana," the courtesans' great numbers, reasons
why they are tolerated, their rooms ("The Paradise of Venus"), makeup, jewelry,
rhetorical skill, and fate as they age, as well as what happens to their babies,
Coryate concludes with a section called "The knowledge of evil is not evil":

> Neither can I be perswaded that it ought to be esteemed for a staine
> or blemish to the reputation of an honest and ingenuous man to see
> a Cortezan in her house, and note her manners and conversation,
> because according to the old maxime, Cognitio mali non est mala,
> the knowledge of evill is not evill, but the practice and execution
> thereof. For I thinke that a virtuous man will be the more

confirmed and settled in virtue by the observation of some vices, then if he did not at all know what they were. For which cause we may read that the aunccient Lacedemonians were wont sometimes to make their slaves drunke, which were called Helotæ, and so present them to their children in the middest of their drunken pangs, to the end that by seeing the uglinesse of that vice in others, they might the more loath and detest it in themselves all the dayes of their life afterward: as for mine owne part I would have thee consider that even as the river Rhodanus (to use that most excellent comparison, that eloquent Kirchnerus doth in his Oration that I have prefixed before this booke) doth passe through the lake Losanna, and yet mingleth not his waters therewith; and as the Fountain Arethusa runneth through the Sea, and confoundeth not her fresh water with the salt liquor of the sea; and as the beames of the Sunne doe penetrate into many uncleane places, and yet are nothing polluted with the impuritie thereof: so did I visite the Palace of a noble Cortezan, view her own amorous person, heare her talke, observe her fashion of life, and yet was nothing contaminated therewith, nor corrupted in maner. Therefore I instantly request thee (most candid reader) to be as charitably conceited of me, though I have at large deciphered and as it were anatomized a Venetian Cortezan unto thee, as thou wouldest have me of thy selfe upon the like request.[21]

Milton's famously erroneous statement, which is frequently cited to support the argument that Guyon behaves temperately, is relevant to Coryate's disclaimer: "Our sage and serious Poet *Spencer*, whom I dare be known to think a better teacher than *Scotus* or *Aquinas*, describing true temperance under the person of *Guion*, brings him in with his palmer through the cave of Mammon, and the bowr of earthly blisse that he might see and know, and yet abstain."[22] By accomplishing the same goal in his visit to Margarita Æmeliana, Coryate avoids what Milton calls "a fugitive and cloister'd virtue."[23] As Milton is aware, it is imperative in the binary universe in which we live to test and define a virtue like temperance by exposure to its opposite, and there can be no better way to test a man's temperance in the Renaissance than to visit a Circe of Venice. "A virtuous man," says Coryate, "will be the more confirmed and settled in virtue by the observation of some vices, then if he did not at all know what they were." Thus he gives himself extremely high marks: on a scale ranging from temperance (a mean between extremes, with reason and desire in harmony: one desires what reason mandates) downward to continence (reason overcoming improper desire), incontinence (desire overcoming reason), and self-indulgence (desire active, reason inactive),[24] Coryate views himself as a temperate man whose virtue is reinforced by habit. He satisfies his curiosity without lapsing into carnal desires; he sees a courtesan and now knows much about her trade, yet his desire is not corrupted.

To the careful reader, however, Coryate's mini-treatise on temperance belies his true and equivocal frame of mind. Other details in the account suggest that the author, rather than being temperate, is merely continent (that the courtesan stirs his desires, which his reason must then overcome). Contrary to Coryate's stated intention, the picture he has "here inserted" reveals conflicting emotions. He and Margarita are inclined toward each other in greeting: she, bedecked in her full working rig, reaches out with her right arm in a partial embrace, beckoning toward her bosom with her left hand, a gesture both of welcome and of sexually provocative invitation; meanwhile, he is evidently striding up to her, holding his right hand over his heart, a gesture both of courtesy and of emotional guardedness. But the major clue to the disharmony between Coryate's purportedly ethnographic intention and his desire for sex with the courtesan is his hat. He concludes the sentence in which he mentions Ulysses's moly by saying that if a man lacks "some antidote against these Venereous titillations, she [the courtesan] will very neare benumme and captivate thy senses, and make reason vale bonet [remove a hat in respect] to affection."[25] The picture shows Signor Tomaso having doffed his hat in gentlemanly respect, but the image of the upturned headgear ironically calls to mind the association Coryate makes with licentiousness. On the other hand, he holds the hat over his genital area as if to protect his sexuality from the wily and willing courtesan. The positions of Coryate's right hand and hat indicate that he is on guard lest he be tempted into incontinence, and the manner in which he holds his hat suggests fear of sexual relations with the courtesan. A single phallic finger reaches over the brim and is dwarfed by the black hole within, raising the specter of male sexual inadequacy in the presence of a woman whose business is the sex trade. One remembers that Odysseus, even after overcoming Circe's charms, still feels the need to make her promise that when they are naked she will not make him feel like a weakling unmanned. Of course, Odysseus beds down with Circe for a year, and Coryate, if one can believe him, remains chaste, but despite differing circumstances they share the fear of emasculation at the hands of a sexual predator.

What Coryate's picture reveals is nicely theorized in Freud's work on taboo. Coryate feels the ambivalence of emotions, which Freud understands as the tension between desire and detestation or fear with respect to a taboo action (in this case, intercourse with a courtesan), for "the basis of taboo is a prohibited action, for performing which a strong inclination exists in the unconscious."[26] Freud specifically addresses the adolescent version of the ambivalence apparent in Coryate's adult journal:

> The boy at the same time gains a knowledge of the existence of certain women who practice sexual intercourse as a means of livelihood, and who are for this reason held in general contempt. The boy himself is necessarily far from feeling this contempt: as soon as he learns that he too can be initiated by these unfortunates into sexual life, which till then he accepted as being reserved exclusively for "grown-ups", he regards them with a mixture of longing and horror.[27]

This tension results in "a need for discharge," which is achieved in "compromise actions"; "from one point of view they are evidences of remorse, efforts at expiation . . . while on the other hand they are at the same time substitutive acts to compensate the instinct for what has been prohibited." He concludes that these acts of compromise move closer and closer to the taboo act.[28]

The point is that Coryate feels, on the one hand, fear of emasculation by Margarita and dishonor in the eyes of his English readers, while on the other his desire and rumors about courtesans so fuel his curiosity that he interviews her as an act of compromise. Visiting "her chamber of recreation" only deepens Coryate's ambivalence: there, he says,

> Thou shalt see all manner of pleasing objects, as many faire painted coffers wherewith it is garnished round about, a curious milke-white canopy of needle worke a silke quilt embrodered with gold: and generally all her bedding sweetly perfumed. And amongst other amiable ornaments she will shew thee one thing only in her chamber tending to mortification, a matter strange amongst so many irritamenta malorum [incitements to evil]; even the picture of our Lady by her bedde side, with Christ in her armes, placed within a cristall glasse.[29]

Her chamber, then, manifests the same duality as Venice itself: amid various enticements arousing desire for the scarlet woman is a picture of God and his mother the Virgin, which cools a client's desire and may make him think twice about physically harming the courtesan or settle for less than he had bargained for, while simultaneously making the sexual encounter more intense by reminding him of its sinfulness.

Rather than being a straightforwardly temperate action manifesting desire for what reason approves, Coryate's visit to the courtesan exemplifies continence: his well-reasoned restraint overcomes his ambivalent desire. The visit is an act of compromise that brings the author, despite his protestations to the contrary, a major step closer to the forbidden act, for as David G. Myers puts it, "The drift toward evil usually comes in small increments, without any conscious intent to do evil."[30]

2. Guyon at Idle Lake

Like Coryate asserting his virtue, some Spenser critics have maintained that Guyon is completely temperate in his brief foray with Phaedria onto Idle Lake. Ernest Sirluck, the first and foremost scholar of Aristotelian philosophy in the poem, states, "In his response to Phaedria's sexual enticement, Guyon represents temperance in the strict Aristotelian sense, the mean with respect to the relevant pleasures of which Cymochles is the excess. . . . Temperance in the strict Aristotelian sense—the mean in respect of the pleasures and pains of touch and taste—is what Guyon represented in his encounters with Phaedria and Cymochles."[31] Or as Lewis H. Miller, Jr., summarizes, "Hamilton and others point to the Phaedria episode as a perfect example of temperance in action."[32]

Phaedria is more than immodest mirth, for Spenser clearly states that she represents "loose dalliaunce," "sensuall delight," and "carelesse ease" (vi.8, 13); she is indeed a "wanton mayd" (vi.40), or a "sexual temptress."[33] Given this association of Phaedria with sexual temptation, it is important to evaluate Guyon's temperance in terms of both the mean and the relationship between reason and desire. Is he temperate or continent? Does he desire the right action, or does reason subdue wrongful desire? The Palmer's absence has been taken to mean that the knight is temperate: if Guyon is not guided by reason and still behaves properly, then he must desire the good and is therefore temperate. The problem with this view, however, is that the Palmer's absence indicates neither the presence of perfected desire nor the absence of all reason. In order to overcome inappropriate desire in the Idle Lake episode, Guyon exerts such reason as he possesses apart from the Palmer's external reinforcement.

Beginning with the headnote, Canto 6 strongly supports a reading of Guyon as continent in the face of sexual temptation: *"Guyon is of immodest Merth, / led into loose desire."* Stanza one begins by identifying continence, not temperance, as the theme of the Idle Lake episode: "A Harder lesson, to learne Continence / In ioyous pleasure, then in grieuous paine." Details about Guyon's attitude also suggest that Canto 6 provides an exemplum of continence. After Phaedria's immodest mirth in stanza 23, Spenser says, "But he halfe discontent, mote nathelesse / Himselfe appease, and issewd forth on shore" (24). If the knight is only "halfe discontent," he must also be half content to land on Phaedria's sensuously provocative island. The next evidence comes in stanza 26:

> But he was wise, and warie of her will,
> And euer held his hand vpon his hart:
> Yet would not seeme so rude, and thewed ill,
> As to despise so courteous seeming part,
> That gentle Ladie did to him impart,
> But fairely tempring fond desire subdewd,
> And euer her desired to depart.

Perhaps the critical misconception about Guyon's temperance stems from this stanza: the fact that he follows a perfect mean in courteous words and behavior does not necessarily signify perfect temperance on the inside. Indeed the stanza shows "his hand vpon his hart," the same gesture of emotional guardedness that Coryate makes in the picture, and if Guyon's desire must be subdued, then it must not be in harmony with his reason. (The presence of "tempring" may be why Sirluck takes the line as evidence of temperance,[34] but that interpretation overlooks the presence of inappropriate desire in the same line.)

The most direct evidence for continence comes in stanza 40 after Guyon and Cymochles fight:

> But sober *Guyon*, hearing him so raile,
> Though somewhat moued in his mightie hart,
> Yet with strong reason maistred passion fraile,
> And passed fairely forth.

He is "somewhat moued" in an inappropriate direction, but reason overcomes "passion fraile." Sirluck's view that Guyon "does not feel the strong desires which the continent man bridles by means of his reason" but "is, instead, the temperate man who feels desire only for the right things" is simply mistaken.[35] Continence and incontinence differ not in the nature of desire but rather in one's response to it: the incontinent man lacks inner restraint and acts on his desire; the continent man, his reason restraining his desire, remains virtuous. If avoiding incontinence does not necessarily mean that one has no inappropriate desires and is therefore temperate, then Sirluck misrepresents Guyon's situation by assuming a harmony of action and emotion.

It should by now be clear, as Spenser himself alerts us, that Guyon's encounter with Phaedria is not a matter of mere "equivocations" with respect to temperance[36] but instead an example of continence in action. At his stage in the development of temperance it is important to test and define virtue against sensual temptation, for such an encounter strengthens positive habits. In the process, the knight manifests what Augustine calls "curiosity, for experiment's sake, [which] seeks the contrary of these,— not with a view of undergoing uneasiness, but from the passion of experimenting upon and knowing them."[37]

The problem with Guyon's sojourn in Canto 6, however, is that curiosity involves not only the positive intention to abstain but also the negative impulse to indulge; the curiosity to see and know swings in contrary directions. Although the knight resists Phaedria's sensual temptation and his mission seems as strictly ethnographic as Coryate's, indulgence with Phaedria, the prostitute-figure, whose lay coincidentally mentions "The Flowre-deluce" in stanza 16, the name of a brothel in medieval Southwark,[38] is just a step away, for as Charles Winick and Paul M. Kinsie remark, "Some prostitutes have a strong curiosity value to customers."[39]

In light of the historical analogue provided by Coryate's visit to the Venetian courtesan, Canto 6 can be viewed as a Freudian act of compromise. Guyon leaves behind the Palmer (the guarantee of resistance to temptation) and decides to take a walk on the wild side yet to abstain from doing anything more than placing himself in a dangerous setting, though the mere fact that he is there in the first place is not completely proper. There is an additional act of compromise within the journey itself: although the immodest mirth and sensuous delight that Guyon spurns fall short of the sensual indulgence to which Cymochles succumbs, they nonetheless point in that general direction. The danger to Guyon is not that he too will succumb to Phaedria's charms, for he is stalwartly continent, but that below the level of conscious restraint the desire for sensual interaction persists in his unconscious where it may have a negative impact on his future actions in the same way that Hawthorne's Young Goodman Brown's resistance does not prevent the sights that he sees in the night woods from blighting the rest of his life. Mature temperance would not need to put itself to the test, nor would there be any desire to do so because a temperate man desires only what reason abides. But if reason does not anchor one to continence, inappropriate desire can lead a man, through incontinence, to wreck his life.

3. Ambivalence and Prostitution

The same Freudian ambivalance in Coryate's chaste visit to a Venetian courtesan exists more generally in the history of prostitution between the forces of desire and the forces of restraint. My purpose here is not to provide a comprehensive history of the topic in medieval and Renaissance London, for this already exists in numerous places,[40] but instead to highlight the theme of ambivalence, which will inform a reading of Canto 12 in terms of prostitution.

The medieval attitude was heavily influenced by Augustine and Aquinas, both of whom viewed prostitution as a necessary evil. "Remove prostitutes from human affairs," Augustine cautioned, "and you will unsettle everything because of lusts," a passage that Aquinas quotes.[41] Ruth Mazo Karras points out that "across [medieval] Europe the authorities saw regulated brothels as a foundation of the social order, releasing tensions that would otherwise lead to sodomy, rape, and seduction."[42] Prostitution, while undesirable in itself, was tolerated because society would have been worse off without it. This reluctant toleration also characterized the strategy of officially sponsoring London stews in Southwark on the southern bank of the Thames in hopes that the city proper would be a cleaner place.[43] As Steven Mullaney points out, prostitution—like the theater—was tolerated on society's margins, halfway between the rule of law within the ancient Roman wall and the lawlessness of the countryside.[44] Perhaps as a partial result of the tolerance expressed by Augustine and Aquinas, there were significant connections between prostitution and the Roman Catholic Church. Besides the centuries-long link between nunneries and prostitution, Popes Sixtus IV and Leo X licensed prostitutes and taxed their earnings.[45] Pope Alexander VI "repeatedly entertained prostitutes in the Vatican palace."[46] In medieval London an English cardinal bought a brothel house and allowed it to continue operating.[47] Priests even kept concubines; "in England, 'couillage' was the name given to the licenses required . . . to keep these women."[48] And the stews "were under the direction of the Bishops of Winchester."[49] So although lechery was considered a deadly sin, the Roman Catholic Church not only allowed prostitution but also benefited from it financially, and some popes and priests even mocked their vow of celibacy by using prostitutes (the origin of Hamlet's pun on "nunery," of course, is that some of the used women were not professional prostitutes but nuns in convents).

Spenser's view of Catholicism as the Whore of Babylon is more than hollow name calling. Besides support by numerous Protestant commentaries on Revelation, there was historical justification: the Church's strong involvement in prostitution, as licensers and clients, gave Spenser good reason to portray the Catholic Church as the whore Duessa. Indeed, "the Catholic Church's vulnerability on sex encouraged its identification as the whore of Babylon."[50] Hamilton considers the possibility that Spenser portrays "Acrasia as the Church of Rome" to be limiting.[51] Certainly she is not exclusively an allegory of the Church, but if the great anti-Gloriana of Book II has things in common with Renaissance prostitution, as I intend to show, then it may be that Spenser's anti-Catholic allegory is not limited to Book I and augments the unity of the 1590 poem.

By the mid-fourteenth century, prostitution was established on the south bank of the Thames,[52] and from then on there were attempts to eliminate or regulate it in 1436, 1460, 1506, and 1535, the latter attempts fueled by the arrival of syphilis in the 1490s.[53] In 1546 Henry VIII closed all the public brothels, but this action merely led to privatization and street walking.[54] The brothels were reopened under Edward VI and continued open under Mary Tudor, though prostitutes were sometimes punished.[55]   Elizabeth's government tried "to check the unrestrained building" of brothels[56] and in 1563 closed the stews but did not "ferret out prostitution in inns and taverns."[57]   The brothel area on the south bank actually expanded in the Elizabethan age, despite a major crackdown in 1576-77.

The problem with these attempts to regulate and eliminate prostitution was that anti-vice law was stubbornly opposed by human nature. Although closing the brothels was in line with the preferences of religious reformers, Hugh Latimer complained in a 1549 sermon about the contradiction between law and lust: "My Lords, you have put down the stews: but I pray you what is the matter amended? . . . Ye have but changed the place, and not taken the whoredome away. . . . I here say there is now more whoredom in London than there was on the Bank."[58] Latimer's comment illustrates Foucault's sense in *The History of Sexuality Volume I* that prohibiting certain sexual activities actually produces the opposite effect by calling attention to them.[59]   As this brief history reveals, prostitution—as a necessary evil, as antithetical to popes' and priests' vow of celibacy, and as the object of ineffectual regulation—was both detested and desired, both persecuted and winked at, much as it is in our own age. In the next section, after showing that prostitution is a workable analogy for Canto 12, I will argue that Guyon's destruction of the Bower reflects the historical ambivalence toward London prostitution just summarized and suggests that his ultimate victory over Acrasia emphasizes continence more than temperance.

4. Spenser's Brothel

Hamilton makes this sunny statement about Canto 12: "When Guyon approaches the Bower, 'now gins this goodly frame of Temperance / Fairely to rise'; now Guyon becomes this image of temperance, of man guided by reason and aided by grace standing against all the temptations of the world, the flesh, and the devil."[60]   Whereas Spenser specifically mentions continence at the beginning of

Canto 6, now in the first line of Canto 12 he indicates that the climax will illustrate Guyon's temperance. The trouble is that certain details deconstruct a neat interpretation such as Hamilton's by suggesting that the knight's actions and reactions participate in the same ambivalence that animates the history of prostitution. In order for this analogy to hold, though, we must first demonstrate that elements of Canto 12 suggest prostitution, especially that there are parallels between Elizabethan brothels and the Bower of Bliss, "where Pleasure dwelles in sensuall delights" (II.xii.1).

Spenser's immediate source for Acrasia is Tasso's Armida in *Jerusalem Delivered*, Books 15-16; however, both temptresses share a common link to Homer's Circe and Calypso, who for C. G. Jung represent a man's anima[61]–that is, they objectify the lust and sloth that are the twin perils arising from a man's psychic disunity. Gareth Roberts notes that while Circe in particular represents the "fear of magical female sexuality," she is also a figure of the prostitute; indeed Horace associates her with a whore, and Petronius sees her as a courtesan.[62] Nor is the Circe-prostitute association lost on James Joyce, who "transforms Circe's magical glen and polished stone hall with its 'shining doors' into Bella Cohen's brothel."[63] Therefore, even if we view Spenser's Acrasia strictly in terms of the epic tradition, prostitution is a viable historical analogy.

To begin with, some elements of Guyon's boat voyage also suggest prostitution. Maurice Evans even refers to "the prostitutes of the floating islands"[64]–Phaedria and the mermaids. Spenser creates five mermaids (versus three in classical myth) in order to stress sensuality's appeal to all of the senses (the brothel's basic seduction strategy). In addition, Guyon's approach to the Bower is after all over water, much as clients had to cross the Thames; in fact, some of the Bankside brothels were so close to the water that they had stairs down to the waterfront for easy access.[65] Although the crossing was riskier than it sounds (it was illegal to cross the river at night in the early sixteenth century),[66] the Thames was not the kind of nautical "*Labyrinth*" (II.xii.20) through which

Guyon must pass (here one remembers that the image suggests sensuality in the Renaissance). Much like the Redcrosse Knight's penetration of the Wood of Errour (error; *errare viā*, to wander from the right path; the wandering islands), reaching the Bower requires an extreme effort of will to negotiate numerous Homeric obstacles.

Like a client going to a Bankside brothel, knights do not merely stumble upon the Bower by accident. In Guyon's case, getting there takes an effort of continence—he and the Palmer work together with the boatman (will). Although in stanza 33 Guyon, in response to the mermaids, "A solemne Meane vnto them measured," in the next stanza "the Palmer from that vanity, / With temperate aduice discounselled." As in the Phaedria episode, Guyon is more attracted to the mermaids than his temperate action suggests; if his reason corrects his desire, then his outer temperance is qualified by an inner state of continence.

The Bankside stews, moreover, were associated with hell in the popular imagination because "the [London] underworld was the image of hell and vice versa."[67] The passage across the Thames was a ride "'over the Styx to Acheron,' as was facetiously said."[68] In Dekker's *Lanthorn and Candelight* (1608), a visitor from hell reacts to the suburbs: "And what saw he there? . . . He saw the doors of notorious carted bawds like Hell gates stand night and day wide open, with a pair of harlots in taffeta gowns, like two painted posts, garnishing out those doors, being better to the house than a double sign." In Dekker's *The Honest Whore* Hippolito says:

> For your body
> Is like the common shore, that still receives
> All the town's filth. The sin of many men
> Is within you; and thus much I suppose,
> That if all your committers stood in a rank,
> They'd make a lane in which your shame might dwell
> And with their spaces reach from hence to hell.

Puritan preacher Philip Stubbs argued in *The Anatomy of Abuses* (1583) that whoredom "brings everlasting damnation to all that live therein to the end without repentance" and that "they who think it such sweet meat here, shall find the sauce sour and styptic enough in hell."[69]   As for hell on earth, syphilis was God's punishment for lechery and a foretaste of torment in hell; for example, Robert Greene writes that the pox is "a thing to be feared as deadly while men live, as Hell is to be dreaded after death."[70]   The biblical analogy may well have been the prostitute mentioned in Proverbs 5:5: "Her fete go down to death, and her steppes take holde on hel."   In a similar way, Spenser describes Guyon's voyage to the Bower in terms that suggest a descent into hell: "that Gulfes deuouring iawes" "seem'd more horrible then hell to bee, / Or that darke dreadfull hole of *Tartare* steepe" (II.xii.4, 6).   If Elizabethans thought of prostitution/sensuality as hell, and if Guyon's voyage toward the sensual Bower echoes this aspect of the London underworld, then prostitution ought to be a reasonable historical analogy for the trials of temperance.

Another chthonic detail appears after Guyon lands on Acrasia's island: the ivory gate with the story of Jason and Medea on it, which "euer open stood to all" like the entrance to the House of Pride (44-6; I.iv.6).   Medea, Circe's niece, "for Conti and others signified *immoderatam libidinem* (excessive lust)."[71]   But by calling to mind Aeneas's exit from the underworld through the gate of false dreams, the ivory gate also suggests that the experience remembered by those who pass through it may be illusory, a deceptive dream.   A more precise link to prostitution is that by the time Henry VIII shut down the stews in 1546 they were painted white (presumably to be visible from the river) and identified by signs,[72] parallel to the ivory and the mythological story depicted on it, both of which portend ill for all who enter.   Moreover, one of the medieval regulations that Stow quotes is that "no man [was] to be drawn or enticed into any stew-house."[73]   I suspect that this law was winked at in its own day and was abandoned by the Elizabethan age.   As for Canto 12, no one forces a knight to pass through the gate.

The Bower itself has numerous similarities to London brothels.   As stanza 59 states, "Art at nature did repine; / So striuing each th'other to vndermine."   Art imitates nature and "as halfe in scorne / Of niggard Nature, like a pompous bride / Did decke her, and too lauishly adorne, / When forth from virgin bowre she comes in th'early morne" (50). The flowers are "painted flowres" (58), and art has so overcome nature that Graziani calls the Bower "Acrasia's glitzy production."[74] Prostitutes are not called "painted women" without reason, and high class brothels often contained art objects in an attempt to give customers the sense that they had stepped into a world of luxury and sensual satisfaction—the same impression Coryate has in the courtesan's chamber of "the prostitutional capacity . . . for the transcendence of nature through representation."[75] Coincidentally, the lay about "the Virgin Rose" sung by Acrasia's servant echoes the Rose, a brothel in medieval Southwark.[76] A stronger piece of evidence is that there is clear physical contact in the Bower ("wanton ioyes," and "kisses light" in stanzas 72 and 73). During a knight's post-coital sleep, Acrasia sucks the spirit through his eyes (73). Sheila T. Cavanagh states, "The knight here displays an emasculated vulnerability similar to Red Cross Knight's unguarded post-coital lethargy. In both cases, and in similar episodes, women demonstrate that they can successfully deplete men of important life fluids."[77] Cavanagh's statement is perhaps more and less than needs to be said about Verdant asleep in Acrasia's lap. Prostitution again furnishes an appropriate analogy. Thomas Nashe writes:

> Positions & instructions haue they, to make theyr whores a hundred times more whorish and treacherous, then theyr owne wicked affects (resigned to the deuils disposing) can make them. Waters and receipts haue they to enable a man to the acte after hee is spent, dormatiue potions to procure deadly sleepe, that when the hackney he hath payde for lies by hym, hee may haue no power to deale wyth her, but she may steale from hym, whiles he is in deepe memento, and make her gayne of three or foure other.[78]

Nashe's statement parallels Acrasia's lulling a knight to sleep and sucking the spirit through his eyes. What she accomplishes is not mere physical debauchery, the theft of money from a dupe, or the lost masculinity that Cavanagh mentions. In Spenser, there is the sense of bodily intercourse with a demon, comparable to

78

what transpires between Doctor Faustus and the demon masquerading as Helen,[79] the result being the loss of a knight's very soul. This comparison strengthens the possibility that Acrasia participates in the religious allegory: intemperance has spiritual consequences even in the realm of moral virtue.

Considered on its own, any of the above details would seem neutral at best, but together they constitute a reasonable case for a man's encounter with prositution as an analogy for Canto 12. As Frye says, such details "co-ordinate and bring into focus a great many [impressions of human life], and this is part of what Aristotle means by the typical or universal human event."[80] Evidence of a more direct sort is the nature and spatial organization of Guyon's encounters on the island. Let us first remember that "the Elizabethan brothel was a place where a man could eat, drink, smoke, hear a lewd song, and—for a price ranging from sixpence to a half crown or so—take his pleasure with a woman."[81] Earlier I pointed out that the brothel's strategy for seducing a man was to appeal to all five senses, and that is precisely what the critic is getting at: a man eats, drinks and smokes (taste and smell); hears a lewd song, presumably sung by a provocative woman (hearing and sight); and he passes on to fornication (all five senses, but especially touch). There is a logical and causal progression among these stages. Drink loosens his inhibitions, and satisfaction of one appetite suggests the imperative of another. The lewd song appeals visually (men are visual creatures, hence the proliferation of pornography in our own age), and a lewd song gets him thinking about a different kind of lay. Having sufficiently lubricated a man's remaining inhibitions, the brothel offers a chance for him to go upstairs with a woman. The ascending order of decadence and danger is a series of acts of compromise culminating in abandonment of inhibitions and engagement in the taboo act of fornication.

Although N. S. Brooke correctly states that Spenser creates three scenes on the island,[82] the critic overlooks the correspondence between the setting and the stages just described. First, Excesse, a "comely dame" "clad in faire weedes, but foule disordered, / And garments loose, that seemd vnmeet for womanhed" (55), offers Guyon a drink; he, like Odysseus in Circe's house, dashes the cup to the ground. So far he is perfectly temperate (desire and reason working together) and embraces St. Paul's advice: "And be not drunke with wine, wherein is excesse; but be fulfilled with the Spirit" (Ephesians 5:18).

Next the knight comes to a fountain (60) where "Two naked Damzelles," also called "wanton Maidens," "wrestle wantonly" (63, 66). Spenser is well aware of the power of such visual stimulation:

> Nought vnder heauen so strongly doth allure
> The sence of man, and all his minde possesse,
> As beauties louely baite, that doth procure
> Great warriours oft their rigour to represse,
> And mighty hands forget their manlinesse;
> Drawn with the powre of an heart-robbing eye,
> And wrapt in fetters of a golden tresse,
> That can with melting pleasaunce mollifye
> Their hardned hearts, enur'd to bloud and cruelty. (V.viii.1)[83]

Against such strong visual stimulation, Guyon is not completely immune: "His stubborne breast gan secret pleasaunce to embrace" (65), "and in his sparkling face / The secret signes of kindled lust appeare" (68). "On which when gazing him the Palmer saw, / He much rebukt those wandring eyes of his, / And counseld well, him forward thence did draw" (69). Reason's active restraint of desire is continence; therefore, Berger's interpretation is a false dichotomy: "The episode dramatizes an awakening of desire rather than an allegory of Reason's triumph."[84] The episode clearly shows reason, in the person of the Palmer, helping Guyon to overcome desire and to resist in the spirit of Proverbs 5:18, which undercuts the beauty of the loose women in the fountain: "Let thy fountaine be blessed, and reioyce with the wife of thy youth."

So far Guyon has encountered the taste and smell of wine, and the visual delights of the naked women. In the third location, the Bower of Bliss proper, he now confronts the temptations of hearing and touch: the lay, and the kisses Acrasia gives to Verdant, who sleeps in her lap (73-75). As a garden, the Bower as a setting for sexual contact calls to mind the use of garden houses "for assignations, as was Angelo's in *Measure for Measure* (IV.i.27-35)."[85] John L. McMullan makes this comment about night houses: "In the better-off areas around Hatton Garden, Pall Mall, and Covent Garden there were fashionable music houses and coffee places which contained concealed interiors with private rooms, parlors, and secret passageways that led into gardens and arbors."[86] In the Elizabethan imagination, then, a carefully concealed natural setting such as the Bower of Bliss would call to mind illicit sexuality and even prostitution.

5. The Razing of the Bower

The seventeenth-century brothel called Holland's Leaguer, which like *Coryat's Crudities* postdated *The Faerie Queene*, is an excellent historical analogue for the Bower's location and structure—Spenser's poem provides a universal image of what Elizabeth Holland's infamous brothel later made concrete and particular. The analogy also enables qualification of Miller's claim "that it is only in the Bower of Bliss that Guyon exhibits true temperance."[87] The historical material, as we shall see, highlights the genuinely equivocal nature of Guyon's temperance.

The place itself had existed as early as 1578 as "a fortified, moated mansion house with gardens in Paris Gardens" on the south bank, and by the 1630s at the latest the same manor was called Holland's Leaguer. It occupied one acre and was surrounded by a moat. The brothel has two obvious similarities to Acrasia's Bower: both are garden settings, and whereas the Bower is on an island, the Leaguer "claimed to be an island out of the ordinary jurisdiction." Like Acrasia's island, then, the Leaguer was hard to get to. In addition to the moat, the Leaguer had a "portcullis, drawbridge . . . and wicket for espial, as well as an armed bully or Pandar to quell disagreeable intruders."[88]

Along with characteristics of its physical location, the Leaguer shares a remarkable fact with the Bower: both were attacked. In 1631-32 the brothel "was besieged by the forces of law and order."[89] In fact, a "leaguer" is a military camp under siege, and Nicholas Goodman's pamphlet *Hollands Leaguer* (1632) is essentially a religious allegory: the madam Britannica Hollandia represents Britain and Holland, the domain of Protestantism in a predominantly Catholic Europe. Seduced, says Goodman, by "one Ignatius, a Puritan Jesuit," Hollandia has become a whore of Babylon, but the forces of Protestantism besiege her establishment in an attempt to bring her back to a middle way. As stated earlier, however, attempts to close the brothels were as ambivalent as they were unsuccessful, and when "the upholders of law and authority" had finished beseiging the Leaguer, the women set up another brothel in Bewdly.[90]

Brothels had also since the fourteenth century been frequent targets of unauthorized raids, perpetrated mainly by apprentices.[91] According to Sir Edmund Chambers, the resulting destruction was not Puritanism in action but the carnivalesque[92]—a momentary reversal of power (the master's as well as the prostitute's) on Shrove Tuesday, a day when license was allowed among London's apprentices. But since apprentices, who "were forbidden to marry until their terms were completed, which usually meant their late 20s,"[93] were often customers at brothels,[94] the vandalizing of bawdy houses and especially the assault on the prostitutes within were ambivalent acts much in the spirit of Freud's insight into violating a taboo:

> The desire to violate it persists in their unconscious; those who obey the taboo have an ambivalent attitude toward what the taboo prohibits. The magical power that is attributed to taboo is based on the capacity for arousing temptation; and it acts like a contagion because examples are contagious and because the prohibited desire in the unconscious shifts from one thing to another. The fact that the violation of a taboo can be atoned for by a renunciation shows that renunciation lies at the basis of obedience to taboo.[95]

In other words, the apprentices' guilt, lust, and frustration—originally focused on violating the fornication taboo—were displaced onto an opposite act of

82

renunciation, and by rioting against the brothels (maintaining the taboo) they manifested emotional ambivalence, a misogynistic desireful hatred.

Lawrence Stone describes a parallel incident that occurred a century after the assault on Holland's Leaguer. In 1731, Mrs. Elizabeth Needham was pilloried, received rough treatment by an angry mob, and died several days later. "It is not known whether the crowd which stoned her to death consisted of women," writes Stone, "or of men anxious to transfer their guilt feelings on to her, but it was probably the latter in light of the comment of the *Grub Street Journal* that 'they acted very ungratefully, considering how much she had done to oblige them.'"[96] As with the apprentice riots, a crowd's act of renunciation (the upholding of law as over against taboo) reveals ambivalent emotions. Put a different way, men destroy what they desire when they cannot control it, and destruction both manifests and compensates for unfulfilled desire.

Guyon's destruction of the Bower of Bliss parallels the above actions against prostitutes:

> But all those pleasant bowres and Pallace braue,
> *Guyon* broke downe, with rigour pittilesse;
> Ne ought their goodly workmanship might saue
> Them from the tempest of his wrathfulnesse,
> But that their blisse he turn'd to balefulnesse:
> Their groues he feld, their gardins did deface,
> Their arbers spoyle, their Cabinets suppress,
> Their banket houses burne, their buildings race,
> And of the fairest late, now made the fowlest place. (83)

This description is so extreme that it is no wonder that Berger calls Guyon's act "a Puritan frenzy." Harriett Hankins makes the same point more gracefully: " . . . as he describes the wrecking of the bower, Spenser shows that puritanical assaults on beauty, poetry, art, and sensuality may themselves take the form of excess. . . ."[97] If Guyon's "rigour pittilesse" and "the tempest of his wrathfulnesse" suggest Puritan extremism and thus a violation of both criteria of temperance (the mean and a harmony of reason and desire), how does the destruction of the Bower fit into the supposed triumph of temperance?

The answer lies in the distinction between destroying the Bower and catching Acrasia in a net. The latter is a mean between the extremes of self-indulgence (Verdant) and the kind of painful and humiliating punishments to which historical prostitutes were subjected.[98] If Guyon and the Palmer work together in stanza 81 as they cast the net over Acrasia, then reason and desire are in "absolute Harmony."[99] But if temperance is thus achieved, Hamilton is incorrect to state that "Acrasia's capture signifies the masculine triumph of reason over the affections which are traditionally feminine,"[100] for that is mere continence, not the harmony of reason and desire. In razing the Bower, however, Guyon acts alone. Like the apprentices who rioted against the London brothels, he exhibits wrathfulness that compensates for its opposite, the lust that flickers in his psyche during the fountain scene. Since destroying the Bower violates the mean, his act is merely continent—a Freudian act of renunciation in which desire is channelled into a nonsexual act that affirms and upholds a taboo. Madelon S. Gohlke expresses the right idea: "The internal pressure of resistance finally erupts into 'the tempest of wrathfulnesse,' into the state of perverted sexual energy which destroys the object of his desire. . . . Guyon's rage against the garden expresses his rage against Acrasia as a betrayer, and against his own sexual nature as a force which undermines from within."[101] The only thing missing from this statement is the historical analogue provided by the apprentices. Guyon's act reflects not only his past and present desire but also an ongoing tendency toward it. Destroying the Bower guards against future weakness because the setting no longer provides an occasion for the exercise of that weakness. Thus Canto 12 culminates not in the achievement of perfect temperance (the overthrow of "all those forces by which the Redcross Knight falls into sin") but in what Laura Mulvey calls the "strange male underworld of fear and desire."[102]

CHAPTER FIVE
MERLIN'S AMBIGUOUS HELL POWER IN BOOK III

Spenser's underworlds, caves, and dungeons in Books I and II suggest not only the error of failing to embrace holiness or temperance but also the punishments that result. Merlin's cave in Book III, Canto 3, has appeared to be an exception to this principle. Certainly there is nothing sinister in Spenser's most direct model, the *Orlando Furioso*, Canto 3, in which Bradamante hears from Melissa about her descendants and later has a long conversation with Merlin. The positive nature of the magician is underscored by William Blackburn, who states that "Spenser's Merlin, though he is well able to command demons, does not resort to them for prophecy—Spenser seems less interested than Ariosto in reminding the reader that no magic is entirely above suspicion." He also says that "Spenser is at constant pains to remind us that Merlin's art is free of diabolism. . . ."[1] In Blackburn's analysis, the poem's magicians are poet-figures, and Merlin is merely the benevolent counterpart of Archimago and Busirane. "In fact," states Patrick Gerard Cheney, "*within the poem* Merlin does not practice magic at all."[2]

Merlin becomes a less positive figure, however, when juxtaposed with Ate or Discord. Ate is a logical foil not only because her own underground dwelling in Book IV, Canto 1, suggests a parallel to Merlin's. More importantly, if Merlin promotes marital union, then his effectiveness must be measured against its adversary, and marriage is indeed one of Discord's favorite targets. In describing the walls of her underground dwelling, Spenser mentions "the bloodie feast, which sent away / So many *Centaures* drunken soules to hell, / That vnder great *Alcides* furie fell" (23).[3] The allusion is to the marriage of Pirithous and

Hippodamia, at which the drunken Centaurs tried to rape the bride. The tragedy of Oedipus and the judgment of Paris, also mentioned, are similar inasmuch as discord is domestic and attempts to disrupt relations between husbands and wives. In Book IV, which culminates in the marriage of the Thames and the Medway, the union of husband and wife is a familiar target. Spenser's first mention of Ate even identifies her as the mythological promoter of marital discord, for it is she who casts the golden apple among the gods (II.vii.55). Thus the description of Ate's dwelling in the 1596 *Faerie Queene* confirms what was already part of Spenser's scheme in 1590. Of course, promoting union in marriage is not the same as promoting harmony within marriage or directly opposing the discord Ate represents. While Merlin helps motivate Britomart to find Artegall, the magician's direct influence never extends beyond the walls of his cave. By contrasting Ate and Merlin, this chapter shows that he is neither a completely effective promoter of marital union and harmony nor an unqualified figure of goodness. Underneath his attractive appearance lurks a demonic side, which deserves further exploration. Ultimately, his ambiguous nature is underscored by Britomart, who shares essential characteristics with both figures and accomplishes more than Merlin chooses to achieve.

1. Versus Ate: A Positive View of Merlin

Nevertheless, sharp contrasts between Ate and Merlin highlight his genuinely positive characteristics. To begin with, Ate's lineage is completely infernal,[4] but Merlin's is only partly so. As the son of a nun and an incubus, he can draw on hell for his magical power, using it to promote harmony without any assistance from divine grace yet without serving the devil.

> And sooth, men say that he was not the sonne
> Of mortall Syre, or other liuing wight,
> But wondrously begotten, and begonne
> By false illusion of a guilefull Spright,

On a faire Ladie Nonne. . . . (III.iii.13)

One legend in which Merlin is baptized immediately after birth suggests that grace is active in his life,[5] but Spenser does not include the detail. Nonetheless, Merlin's attitude toward God contrasts markedly with Ate's. Whereas "euen th'Almightie selfe she did maligne" (IV.i.30), Merlin urges reverence and submission to God: "Therefore submit thy wayes vnto his will," he counsels Britomart (III.iii.24).

Ate's family tree includes Night, and Merlin can alter the course of day and night, or at least what is both Night's descendant and one of her manifestations, darkness and the blindness to which it leads.

> For he by words could call out of the sky
> Both Sunne and Moone, and make them him obay:
> That land to sea, and sea to maineland dry,
> And darkesome night he eke could turne to day. (III.iii.12)

In spite of Merlin's demonic lineage, his "magic finds its ultimate source in Christian miracle" because the lines relate to I.x.20 where Fidelia is said to possess similar powers over the sun, the mountains, and the sea—abilities that call to mind biblical passages attributing great powers to the faithful.[6] Spenser's statement on Merlin's magic is also significant if "the forest, the sea, and the night of Books 3 and 4 are the underworld of the poem as a whole,"[7] for in stanza 12 Spenser stresses Merlin's control over two of these elements. His power over night is especially positive because Night is among the most elemental hell powers in *The Faerie Queene*, second only to her father Demogorgon.[8] Although Merlin's power stems from hell itself, he controls day and night for his own purposes, many of which are presumably in line with God's will for his children. Merlin commands a demonic force, rather than being subject to it, and his power, at least potentially, serves the good of human characters.

The constructive use of language in Merlin's alteration of day and night, which contrasts with Ate's use of language to promote discord,[9] makes him a poet-figure, as does his use of magical power to create objects for human use. Besides making the magical mirror and overseeing the brazen wall's construction, Merlin creates a garden mentioned in *The Ruines of Time* (523) and makes Arthur's arms and armor, which Merlin takes to Fairy Land where one who searches can see them (I.vii.36). The interpretation of Merlin as an artist focuses mainly on his creation of the mirror, which Spenser likens to "a world of glas," a microcosm that projects true images, as Spenser conveys poetic truths in the poem (III.ii.19). Merlin thus contrasts with Archimago, a poet-figure who projects falsehood. Both magicians use infernal power to affect the lives of other characters, and together they illustrate what A. Bartlett Giamatti calls the contrasting drives for "revelation" and "self-deception," or for good and evil, within each person.[10] In the interaction of one's positive and negative sides, which Merlin and Archimago represent, the artist finds the genesis of creative work. As the positive side of this duality, Merlin would seem to be not just an exception to the infernal power Ate represents but also her antithesis. Insofar as he wields his power for constructive purposes, Merlin highlights Ate's destructive intent.

As a wielder of infernal power, Merlin also appears positive by contrasting with Archimago and Busirane, poet-figures who use black magic to promote discord. Like the witch who creates the false Florimell by using a sprite to animate a mass of snow molded in her image, Archimago sends a sprite to fetch a false dream from Morpheus's house to trouble the sleeping Redcrosse knight. In contrast, Merlin sets his sprites to a constructive task, building a wall of brass around Cairmardin, which calls to mind other images in the poem—the scales and tower of Book I, the door of Busirane's torture chamber, and the pillar to which he chains Amoret. All of these images recall the gates of hell, where the Old Testament righteous are held captive until Christ liberates them.[11] In the harrowing of hell tradition, the gates of hell fly open in response to the mere will of Christ, who—at least in the view of some sixteenth-century commentators cited in Chapter Four—wields the full power of the Godhead at that moment. In *The Faerie Queene* brazen images call to mind Christ's descent into hell and remind the reader that human beings are in thrall to demonic forces and need divine deliverance. In Book III, Canto 3, however, Merlin's actions contrast with those of Christ. Rather than using divine power to break through brazen gates, Merlin uses infernal power to force hell fiends to build a brazen wall whose very construction ensures their own bondage and whose circular shape may recall the walls around hell itself.

Binding the sprites to their task also makes Merlin a contrast to Archimago and Busirane. Unlike Archimago's assaults on holiness or Busirane's on chastity, preventing sprites from roaming Fairy Land is a clear boon to human beings. What overcomes hell power in Book III, Canto 3, then, is not divine assistance but infernal might, and Merlin's brazen wall marks the bondage of demons rather than of human souls. The hell fiends are now the slaves, not the enslavers, and the construction of the wall is a clear example of Merlin's ability to use hell power without being subject to its influence. His power is so complete, in fact, that the fear he instills in his sprites endures long after his death: "Nath'lesse those feends may not their worke forbeare, / So greatly his commaundement they feare" (iii.11). Whereas Ate engenders disorder and chaos, Merlin forces hell fiends to create a structure somewhat like the spherical mirror, a circular wall whose shape symbolizes order, harmony, and marriage. Such use of hell power rather than grace to curb the forces of discord makes Merlin unique in all of *The Faerie Queene*.

2. A Darker View of Merlin

For all of Merlin's positive contrasts to Ate, Archimago, and Busirane, Spenser does not depict him in entirely positive ways. To begin with, Merlin's epic role in promoting Britomart's desire for marital union, while helpful, is flawed in the same manner as the prophecy Aeneas receives in the underworld from his father Anchises. Although the prophecy fires Aeneas with zeal to fulfill his destiny, it does not include advice on how to proceed. Whereas Britomart's purpose in visiting Merlin's cave is to learn how to find Artegall, the magician provides something altogether different, a prophecy of her descendants.

A perplexing question is whether the prophecy is actually visual or merely verbal. On the one hand, the headnote to Canto 3 mentions that Merlin "*shewes the famous Progeny*" (my emphasis). He says in stanza 32, "Behold the man, and tell me *Britomart*, / If ay more goodly creature thou didst see," and in 50 "other ghastly spectacle [him] dismayd, / That secretly he saw, yet note discoure." One possibility, then, is that the prophecy is Merlin's running commentary on the imagery that he, Britomart, and Glauce all see and that at its conclusion there is something demonic visible only to him. On the other hand, Spenser never explicitly states that images accompany the narration or, if they do, that the women see them. Unlike the prophecies of Melissa in the *Orlando Furioso* and Anchises in the *Aeneid*, Merlin's words may be unaccompanied by images; he may be the only character who can see them; or, overcome by prophetic power, he may be unaware that the prophecy is not visual at all. Thus "Behold the man" can be read in a number of ways including authorial oversight (Spenser forgot that the prophecy is not visual or neglected to say that it is) and imagery that may or may not be visible to the human characters.

However one understands the visual dimension of the prophecy, the important point is that Merlin does not help Britomart find Artegall. When Glauce asks for directions in stanza 25, Merlin says that they will be guided by "mens good endeuours," and in Canto 4, stanza 4, Britomart learns about Artegall from Redcrosse. Whereas Merlin resembles Anchises in never addressing the details of the quest, Glauce, who travels with Britomart, much as the Sibyl journeys with Aeneas through the underworld, does play an advisory role. Spenser's model for the interaction of Britomart and Glauce in Canto 3, however, is Virgil's *Ciris*, in which the nurse Carme attempts to advise Scylla on her love of her father's enemy Minos.[12] As sources for the episode, both the *Aeneid* and the

Ciris underscore the absence of practical assistance on Merlin's part.

A possible objection arises in stanza 51 in regard to the reaction of Britomart and Glauce:

> Then, when them selues they well instructed had
> Of all, that needed them to be inquird,
> They both conceiuing hope of comfort glad,
> With lighter hearts vnto their home retird;
> Where they in secret counsell close conspird,
> How to effect so hard an enterprize,
> And to possesse the purpose they desird:
> Now this, now that twixt them they did deuise,
> And diuerse plots did frame, to maske in strange disguise.

"Then, when them selues they well instructed had / Of all, that needed them to be inquird" certainly sounds as if Merlin offers detailed advice on their journey. But the two lines are ambiguous. What do the two women inquire about—the quest or merely the details of the prophecy? If Merlin does provide Melissa-like advice on how to proceed, Britomart and Glauce ought to conceive more than "hope of comfort glad," and there would be no reason why "they in secret counsell close conspird, / How to effect so hard an enterprize." Nor, if Merlin had shown them the way, would there be any need for Glauce to conceive "a bold deuise" in stanza 52. For Britomart, the main benefit of her visit to Merlin's cave is not a set of directions but her increased desire to find Artegall—desire manifested not only as the kind of zeal Anchises's prophecy inspires in Aeneas but also as the new awareness, symbolized by her blush in stanza 20, of her own role in the process of sexual generation,[13] the womb-like cave being rife with birth imagery.[14]

Although effective in these important ways, the visit to Merlin's cave does not directly help Britomart achieve her immediate goal, locating Artegall. As Spenser portrays him, Merlin is Anchises-like in prophecy, but he does not achieve the advisory function of the Sibyl, Melissa, or Carme. There is a difference between endorsing marriage and actively helping Britomart find Artegall, and on the latter score Merlin falls short. Although he prophesies a future that includes the marital union Ate attempts to spoil, he remains passively focused on his own art. In other words, the human world comes to Merlin, who does not affect it in immediate and concrete ways, but with disruptive intent Ate actively enters the realm of human events. In an exception to C. S. Lewis's general claim that "in *The Faerie Queene* evil does not usually appear as energy,"[15] Ate, the image of evil, is more vigorous than Merlin, the image of relative goodness.

Along with revealing Merlin's passive role in promoting marital union, the prophecy conveys a dark implication about his own nature. The prophecy moves toward the morally ambiguous martial action of one Christian nation against another,[16] which corresponds to a similar moral ambiguity within the seer himself, the latter made possible by the Arthurian context with which Spenser's readers would have been familiar. The presence of Prince Arthur in the poem and the specific mention of the Lady of the Lake and Uther Pendragon in Canto 3 invite such a reading (10, 52). For Spenser and his Elizabethan readers, the Merlin who receives Britomart in Canto 3 would have called to mind the legendary magician who enables King Uther to seduce Igraine, a married woman; who claims the child born of this adultery, Arthur, as the price of his service; who, like Archimago, is a shape shifter; and whose love of the Lady of the Lake renders him unable to save King Arthur from death at the hands of his nephew Mordred. Merlin, whose moral ambiguity is part of Arthurian legend, is a proper conduit for a prophecy that includes morally ambiguous currents, so that the prophecy becomes an extension and a reflection of Merlin's nature. Moreover, his susceptibility to the Lady of the Lake makes him not only a participant in the transience his chronicle includes but also a microcosm of the passing of the Round Table and an emblem of the decay of an age. Even if the prophecy has a positive effect on Britomart, Spenser's Merlin is not only the seer who reveals the workings of divine providence for the English people but also a legendary figure who, by omission or commission, plays a role in the discord within that history. While Merlin helps legitimate the desire that drives Britomart toward union with

Artegall, the magician is indifferent to Artegall's violent end, prophesied in stanza 28. Merlin can foster union but chooses neither to promote harmony within marriage nor to protect it from external harm.

Merlin's art itself is also ambiguous because it is not entirely free of diabolism. Certainly Merlin restrains the hell fiends at work in the cave, but he also "counseld with his sprights" (III.iii.7); the phrase recalls Lucifera, who seeks the "strong aduizement of six wisards old" (I.iv.12). Perhaps the detail in stanza 7 is meant to show Merlin as a positive contrast to Lucifera—able to communicate with demons without sharing their malevolent intentions. On the other hand, communicating with fiends, however positive one's intentions, is as ambiguous as Guyon's self-exposure to temptation in Mammon's cave. There is nothing to suggest that either figure is corrupted, but, as Chapter Four suggests, putting oneself in contact with demonic forces is a morally ambiguous act, however strong one's resistance remains. A similar ambiguity may also be found in the prophecy itself.

> But yet the end is not. There *Merlin* stayd,
> As ouercomen of the spirites powre,
> Or other ghastly spectacle dismayd,
> That secretly he saw, yet note discoure:
> Which suddein fit, and halfe extatick stoure
> When the two fearefull women saw, they grew
> Greatly confused in behauioure;
> At last the fury past, to former hew
> Hee turnd againe, and chearefull looks as erst did shew. (III.iii.50)

There are three possible explanations for Merlin's silence. First, although he does not *resort* to demons for his prophecy of Britomart's progeny, he is clearly in league with hell's forces, draws on hell's power and even momentarily appears to be "ouercomen of the spirites powre." Second, as mentioned above, he may be dismayed by "other ghastly spectacle . . . / That secretly he saw"—either a hell scene or some future human event that would extend the prophecy. Either way one reads the stanza, the magician's state is described as a "fit" and a "fury," which unsettles Britomart and Glauce until his "chearefull looks" return. While Merlin, as the son of a nun and an incubus, wields hell power without serving the devil (and probably uses magic to achieve this end), he appears to be temporarily overcome, one way or another, by the infernal power on which he draws. A third possibility arises from the word "As" in line 2, which signals the uncertainty of Spenser's narrator in determining the source of Merlin's silence. It is only *as if* he is overcome by "spirites powre" or dismayed by "ghastly spectacle"; the real reason behind his trance is mysterious and may still remain unspecified—perhaps demonic, perhaps not.

As Merlin is not completely immune to dark forces during his prophecy, neither is his power a lasting bulwark against discord. Although he fires Britomart with zeal to find Artegall, his prophecy directly benefits only her. Helping Britomart does not imply that Merlin achieves a victory over the forces of hell in a lasting or widespread fashion. After Canto 3 his power does not extend beyond the walls of his cave, and elsewhere in the poem it merely resides in the devices he creates—Arthur's arms and armor, and the magic mirror. Spenser's Merlin, rather than ever directly combating the forces of hell outside his cave in Fairy Land, remains focused on his art like a poet who lives a contemplative life. Yet his future departure from the cave, motivated by his love for the Lady of the Lake, will lead to his demise. Although Merlin's control over the sprites continues after his death, the narrator sounds an ominous note. If you come this way in the present day, he advises the reader, "dare thou not . . . in any cace, / To enter into that same balefull Bowre, / For fear the cruell Feends should thee vnwares deuowre" (8). Travellers in a later age will have to face the kind of dangers Merlin holds in check while he is alive. In the future, the completion of the brazen wall will loose the fiends to roam the earth. Whereas the immortal Ate freely wanders through Fairy Land, Merlin's power has limits not only in its geographical range but also in its effectiveness over time. Spenser never says that Merlin *promotes* discord, but he does not directly use his power to combat it. In light of this distinction, any stress on the contrast between Spenser's living Merlin and Ariosto's Merlin, a mere voice issuing from the tomb, deserves qualification. For all the delight of Canto 3, Spenser's Merlin is ultimately more like the disembodied voice in the *Orlando Furioso* than one at first suspects: effective in enhancing the zeal of his human visitor, but incapable of any direct challenge to the forces of discord.

3. Merlin's Inadequacies and Britomart's Strengths

Although Merlin clearly contrasts with Ate in numerous ways and increases Britomart's desire for the marriage that he does not directly enable, he is neither a completely effective promoter of harmony nor an unambiguous opponent of discord. Of course, Ate is a personification of a moral quality, while Merlin is a person, but allegorically discord is malevolent and active, whereas harmony is benevolent but passive. If a poet-figure, Merlin never gives his works a proper reading, and to the public challenge by Discord he presents a private and inadequate response—the self-interest Britomart must avoid in order to found a line of kings.

The magician's inadequacies become even more clearly focused in light of Britomart's productive mingling of benevolent intention and purposeful action. Like a poet she is a dynamic fallen self, subject to error but able to promote virtue.[17] Insofar as vulnerability enables and defines strength, the Fall becomes fortunate. Like other great victories in *The Faerie Queene*, the liberation of Amoret from Busirane's dungeon, as we will see in Chapter Six, can only be accomplished by one who may fail; the human susceptibility to lust that could cause a lapse of virtue makes victory possible, necessary, and meaningful. There would otherwise be no value in the defeat of Busirane. Fully human and fully tempted, Britomart achieves what Merlin does not: active opposition to Busirane, a force of discord, and (in the 1590 edition at least) the successful reunion of Amoret and Scudamore. Merlin, who is only part human and not fully subject to the Fall, is "an infernal parody of Christ" because they have contrasting fathers, divine and demonic.[18] But more importantly, Merlin parodies Christ because he does not put his power to good use by mounting an active challenge to discord in Fairy Land. He uses it mainly in ways that further his own interests, rather than promoting harmony among all persons or even helping Britomart to find Artegall. Britomart transcends Merlin by effectively promoting concord, but the final measure of his inadequate opposition to discord is the transience of his power. In *The Faerie Queene*, it is characters representing infernal forces who endure (Duessa, Acrasia, Ate) despite the momentary victories of human knights. The assistance Merlin provides is individual, not corporate, and unlike Ate he will ultimately pass away.

CHAPTER SIX

BRITOMART AND THE DESCENT INTO HELL IN BOOKS I-III

By announcing at the beginning of Book II that what follows will be a "like race to runne" (i.32), Spenser signals the fundamental similarities between Guyon's journey and that of the Redcrosse Knight. Whether Spenser's point applies to Britomart's experiences in Book III, however, remains an open question, especially since, in the full 1596 version, the book is easily paired with Book IV in the poem's romance center. But in 1590 that pairing was not possible. One is impelled to ask, then: in what way does Britomart's progress from the magic mirror to Busirane's castle recapitulate the structure and psychology found in Books I and II?

It is clear, to begin with, that the presence of underworlds unifies Books I and II: classical set pieces below the House of Pride and within Mammon's cave, and numerous episodes that echo Christ's harrowing of hell—Redcrosse's victory over Errour, Arthur's rescue of Redcrosse from Orgoglio's dungeon, the dragon fight, Guyon's three-day journeys through Mammon's cave and to the Bower of Bliss, and his victory over Acrasia. Classical and Christian paradigms are equally present in Spenser's imagination and are sometimes blended. In Book II, for example, Spenser places Pilate and Tantalus side by side in Mammon's cave; Guyon enters the Bower through an ivory gate, which appropriately recalls the gate of false dreams through which Aeneas leaves the underworld in *Aeneid* VI; and the knight then casts a net over Acrasia, much as Christ binds Sin and Death in the harrowing of hell tradition.

If the descent into hell is a major aspect of Guyon's "like race," the descent motif may unify not only the first two books but also the remainder of the 1590 edition of *The Faerie Queene*. I do not agree with Thomas E. Maresca that "descent-illumination-ascent," in terms of a Neoplatonic encounter with the body, is both the macrostructure of the poem and the microstructure of a knight's journey.[1] The former is problematic, for it imposes a complete pattern on an unfinished poem. The latter is more nearly valid, but a twofold pattern is more fundamental: descent to underworlds, caves, or places of captivity structures the movement of Redcrosse, Guyon, and Britomart from inexperience to experience—initiation, then victory. As Maresca puts it in *The Spenser Encyclopedia*, "Figuratively each hero is first harrowed from hell and then goes on to harrow hell."[2] In the epic tradition, the pattern is somewhat different: departure, initiation, and return.[3] In *The Faerie Queene*, however, the departure is retrospectively mentioned in the Letter to Ralegh, the knights never return to Cleopolis, and descent is a matter of both initiation and triumph. In fact, the absence of an extended classical underworld in Book III brings the dyad into clearer focus: stripped of geographical or architectural reference points, the descent is really a psychological phenomenon. From encounters with their own shortcomings knights gain the strength for qualified victory over their weaknesses ("qualified" because human fallibility abides even in the presence of mature virtue). Specifically, Redcrosse moves from Errour to the Dragon, Guyon from Phaedria and Mammon to Acrasia, and Britomart from Merlin to Busirane. Unlike Guyon, Britomart does not descend into hell—Book III contains no extended classical underworld as in Book I, Canto 5, or Book II, Canto 7. But, as with Redcrosse, her visits to places within the earth or of confinement are key moments in her psychological development. Her journey in Book III is a "like race" in terms of classical-Christian descent and the psychological development it represents.

Before considering Maresca's theory more closely, I will respond to the objection that Britomart's initiation really involves Malecasta, not Merlin. Canto 1 lacks any specific association with hell, the underworld, the labyrinth, dungeons, and structures of ivory or brass—images that signal moments of initiation or victory elsewhere. Moreover, if Britomart's encounter with Merlin plays *any* role in her sexual initiation, as it surely does, then Malecasta versus Merlin is a false dichotomy. But does Malecasta *also* participate in initiating the knight of chastity? To begin with, Book III, Canto 1, parodies Guyon's visit to the Bower of Bliss, for both Acrasia and Malecasta appeal to male lust (Book III thus begins where Book II ends, and the prerequisite for chastity is the perfection of temperance). Britomart is unmoved, displaying temperance in action—a harmony of reason and desire. By affirming her path toward Artegall and denying lust for a woman, she achieves the ideal resistance to temptation that Guyon should manifest in the Bower. If there is no weakness or capitulation involved in Britomart's encounter with Malecasta, then the latter does not play the role of initiator, for initiation involves an encounter with the inner weakness that a knight must overcome.

It is possible, however, that being wounded by Gardante in Canto 1, stanza 65, does play some role in Britomart's initiation. Certainly her "drops of purple bloud" anticipate the imagery of menstruation and blushing discussed below, but both images are more relevant to Merlin's cave than to Malecasta or even Gardante. If the nick signals a weakness that is confronted more fully in later cantos, Canto 1 prefigures, rather than portrays, Britomart's initiation. Her presence at Malecasta's, therefore, is a hinge connecting the knight of chastity to Redcrosse (who accompanies her) and to Guyon (through temperate response to sensual temptation). The full force of her initiation comes in Canto 3.

1. The Garden of Adonis and Merlin's Cave

Although the absence of a classical underworld in Book III has left the descent more open to interpretation than in previous books, one may seriously question Maresca's Neoplatonic reading, particularly its relation to the Garden of

Adonis. "In the center of the poem as we have it," he writes of the 1596 *Faerie Queene*, "Books 3 and 4 depict the deepest penetration of the *descensus*, the overt encounter with matter and the principle of generation (physical generation of course) and their domination by spirit." Maresca considers the Garden of Adonis to be this "deepest penetration": "What the entire garden presents is the relation of spiritual substance (soul, whether conceived as vegetative, animal, or rational) to matter, and matter itself as the principle of change in opposition/complement to the constancy of spirit."[4]

It is true, of course, that the Garden of Adonis concerns "the nature of corporeality and its relation to spirit."[5] But the descent metaphor does not hold because the Garden of Adonis is not an underworld in terms of "matter" or in any other way. It is a sinless world where souls have yet to receive bodies; a realm of forms outside the material world where souls exist between incarnations; a realm of preexistence, of matterless form, set against the chaos of formless matter outside.[6] Indeed, one of the stanzas Maresca quotes in support of his thesis—it begins "All things from *thence* doe their first being fetch" (III.vi.37 [my emphasis])—refers to the realm outside the Garden mentioned in the previous stanza:

> For in the wide wombe of the world there lyes,
> In hatefull darkenesse and in deepe horrore,
> An huge eternall *Chaos*, which supplyes
> The substances of natures fruitfull progenyes. (III.vi.36).[7]

Elizabeth Bieman quotes the first four lines of stanza 36 in order to reach a different conclusion:

> Daily they grow, and daily forth are sent
> Into the world, it to replenish more;
> Yet is the stocke not lessened, nor spent,
> But still remaines in euerlasting store.

Arguing that the location of matter is equivocal, she concludes, "The 'stock' pile must be in the Garden if its function is to 'replenish' the outside world, yet the stockpile has been located equivocally 'in' the world's 'wide wombe.'"[8] But she misses the fact that "they" in line one refers not to matter but to the Neoplatonic forms in the previous stanza: "Infinite *shapes* of creatures there are bred, / And vncouth *formes*, which none yet euer knew" (my emphasis). These shapes and forms are clearly distinct from the "*substances* of natures fruitfull progenyes," which Chaos supplies (my emphasis). Thus the world outside the Garden of Adonis, rather than the Garden itself, is the realm of bodily generation where spirit and matter unite. In a similar way, the "rocky Caue" (vi.48) underneath the mountain around which the Garden is situated has been taken as a symbol of the world.[9]

The Garden of Adonis, then, is a paradise, not a hell; bodily generation takes place somewhere outside the Garden, not in the Garden itself; and since souls shed their flesh when they arrive and are clothed in flesh only when they leave, the Garden, while part of a process that includes bodily generation, can have nothing to do with descent if the deepest part of the *descensus* is equated with the body.

In a different way, however, the Garden of Adonis may still relate somewhat to a descent, not into a hell but perhaps into some afterlife realm, which in a classical context could only be Elysium. If so, the Garden may be a secular counterpart to the Redcrosse knight's vision of the New Jerusalem on the Mount of Contemplation: the straightforward depiction of afterlife-sainthood versus the course of departed souls and the mechanics of reincarnation. In particular, the chthonic nature of the episode echoes Anchises's stress on the reincarnation of the souls of his future descendants:

> All the rest, when they have passed time's circle
> for a millennium, are summoned by
> the god to Lethe in a great assembly
> that, free of memory, they may return
> beneath the curve of the uper world, that they
> may once again begin to wish for bodies. (VI.988)

Anchises describes the nature of this return to earth earlier in the same passage:

> They are dulled by harmful bodies, blunted

by their own earthly limbs, their mortal members.
Because of these, they fear and long, and sorrow
and joy, they do not see the light of heaven;
they are dungeoned in their darkness and blind prison.
(VI.965-69)[10]

If the descent into hell, as Thomas J. J. Altizer argues, involves a migration from a
higher state to a lower state as in birth, then it is possible to view Christ's descent
in the same fashion: his descent was not really anything that happened during or
after the crucifixion, as sixteenth-century commentators argued, but instead the
incarnation itself.[11]

Although problematic in terms of the Garden of Adonis, Maresca's system
does to a degree illuminate Britomart's visit to Merlin's cave, a connection on
which the critic is silent. Britomart visits the magician ostensibly to discover
Artegall's whereabouts, but her descent into the womb-like cave where she sees a
vision of her descendants leads, as Nohrnberg points out, to an awakening to her
own sexuality symbolized by her "bleeding bowels" (ii.39) and "her blushing"
(iii.20).[12] Nevertheless, a Platonic reading of Canto 3 stressing Britomart's
descent into, or at least a new awareness of, her own body is not sufficient to
understand her twin "descents"—her visit to Merlin's cave and her victory over
Busirane in his "dungeon deepe" (xi.16). These episodes, however, nicely fit the
initiation-victory dyad. Like other descents in *The Faerie Queene*, her visit to
Merlin's cave is an initiation that highlights weakness. Descending in a
metaphorical sense, she confronts not only her own sexual nature but also the
solipsistic, fantasy-driven lust (later embodied by Busirane) that she must
overcome in order to affirm married chastity. The blush, then, makes the episode
parallel to the Redcrosse knight's battle with Errour, for he simultaneously
commits and defeats error; and to Guyon's time with Phaedria and perhaps also
his journey with Mammon if the Knight of Temperance simultaneously shows
curiosity and resists temptation. More broadly, visiting Merlin serves the same
function as Aeneas's past error with Dido and Dante's vision of his own

sinfulness: Merlin is to Britomart as Anchises is to Aeneas, or as Virgil is to Dante.

As these last references suggest, the learning experience is a fundamental characteristic of the descent into hell in the epic tradition: descent provides information about the future and strengthens positive qualities, sometimes by confrontation with what must be overcome. As Charles A. Huttar notes, the purpose of descent is "to prepare the hero as he develops strength of character or gains information needed for heroic deeds he is destined to perform."[13] In the epic tradition, Odysseus becomes the first to seek information in the realm of the dead when he journeys to the asphodel meadow at the end of the world to consult Teiresias. The key element that the seer reveals is not information about logistics (Circe also counsels him about his journey) but the fact that "death will come to you from the sea, in / some altogether unwarlike way, and it will end you / in the ebbing time of a sleek old age."[14] Knowing that he is not destined to waste away in illness or sorrow and seeing the woeful state of Achilles prepare Odysseus to reject immortality, which Calypso later offers, and enable a restorative return to his family and a whole-hearted embrace of mortal life. Similarly, the key element of Aeneas's descent is the major strengthening of his character and of his zeal to bring about the events Anchises foretells. Both Odysseus and Aeneas receive information, but Aeneas's descent is the more psychologically significant. Dante's descent is even more psychological than its classical antecedents, for it involves a direct confrontation with the full spectrum of human shortcomings and their consequences in the afterlife—a confrontation that is a necessary prelude to the spiritual regeneration symbolized by the pilgrim's entry, with the help of grace, into Paradise. It is the employment of these twin purposes—the gathering of information and the achieving of psychological/spiritual development—that makes Spenser's treatment of the underworld in Book III and throughout the 1590 poem heir to the epic tradition.

2. The House of Busirane

As these classical and Christian references suggest, Britomart's early experience can be understood as education or initiation rather than as a reflection of a Neoplatonic theory of descent. In *The Faerie Queene*, those who descend and return become rescuers who embody the main type of descent that Spenser weaves throughout the first three books of the poem: Christ's harrowing of hell. An initiate in Merlin's cave, Britomart becomes a Christ-like liberator when she achieves a qualified triumph by rescuing Amoret from Busirane's house, which is clearly meant to resemble hell.[15] The entrance is blocked by a wall of flame giving off sulphurous smoke, Busirane (unlike Merlin) puts fiends to negative use, and Amoret is chained in darkness (hell, in patristic tradition, is dark in order to deny comfort to the damned).[16] Of course, her trek through the house's three rooms resembles Aeneas's walk through Hades and Guyon's walk through Mammon's cave. Like Guyon she encounters visual delights whose purpose is to subvert virtue, and like Redcrosse as well as Aeneas she encounters allegorical personifications. But Christ's harrowing of hell is equally present in the background of the episode. The Maske of Cupid is preceded by an earthquake, and in stanza 37 Britomart "gan perceiue the house to quake." The earthquake in Matthew 27:51, which rends the curtain of the temple after Christ dies, can be taken as a sign of his descent into hell: "And beholde, the vaile of the Temple was rent in twayne, from the top to the bottome, and the earth did quake, and the stones were clouen." (The destruction anticipates the passage in the *Inferno*, Canto 11, where it is nearly impossible to descend further because of rubble resulting from the earthquake when Christ died.) Doors fly open in a violent storm—a romance motif but also a recollection of Christ's effect on the gates of hell, which respond to the power of his will rather than to any physical force (xii.27). Similarly, the door to the dungeon, which like the gates of hell is made of brass, yields without effort on her part. "That brasen doore flew open, and in went / Bold *Britomart*, as she had late forecast, / Neither of idle shewes, nor of false charmes aghast" (xii.29). The destruction of the brazen pillar in Canto 12, stanza 37, is a further indication that hell's forces are being subdued.

Britomart's time in the house itself may not equal three days, but the total journey, starting with her departure from Scudamore and ending with his reunion with Amoret, does appear to fit that time frame. Long overlooked by everyone except Harold L. Weatherby,[17] this controversial detail deserves supporting explication. Her journey begins in Canto 11, it is "euentyde" in stanza 55, and nightfall of the first day occurs in Canto 12, stanza 1. In the next stanza, the period "from the fourth houre of night vntill the sixt" refers to the pre-dawn hours of the second day. "The morrow next" is finally reached in stanza 28, and in 29 "all that day she outwore in wandering" until we reach "the second euening." It is now "the second watch," the period between 9:00 p.m. and midnight. The battle with Busirane, the destruction of the pillar, and the liberation of Amoret take place. There are no other temporal references in the canto, but imagery visible only in daylight suggests that Britomart's journey, like that of Christ in the underworld, concludes on the morning of the third day.

> Returning backe, those goodly roomes, which erst
> She saw so rich and royally arayd,
> Now vanisht vtterly, and cleane subuerst
> She found, and all their glory quite decayd,
> That sight of such a chaunge her much dismayd. (42)

Finally Britomart must also find Scudamore where she left him, and "*at last* she came vnto the place" (43, my emphasis), implying that additional time has elapsed. It follows that the reunion occurs on the third day of Britomart's journey, which recalls not only Christ's harrowing of hell but also Redcrosse's three-day dragon fight, as well as Guyon's three-day walk through the underworld of Mammon's cave and his three-day boat journey to the Bower of Bliss.

Spenser's equation of Britomart's rescue of Amoret with Christ's harrowing of hell also involves the role of heavenly grace, an echo of Book I's reminder (discussed in Chapter One) that no one returns from hell without divine assistance. Referring to "deepe *Auernus* hole," Spenser states that "there creature neuer past, / That backe returned without heauenly grace" (I.v.31). When Scudamore relates Amoret's situation to Britomart, she urges him to have faith in God: "Yet if that heauenly grace some good reliefe / You send, submit you to high prouidence" (III.xi.14). Like Christ's descent into hell, the rescue is an act of divine grace and is also associated with light—"the shining ray, / With which faire *Britomart* gaue light vnto the day" (i.43).[18] In an indirect way, Britomart not only brings Amoret up to the light but also brings light to a hell-like place of captivity, where she binds Busirane as the Palmer casts a net over Acrasia; or as Christ, the light of the world, descends into the unlit reaches of hell to free the Old Testament righteous and to bind Sin and Death: "Thou art gone vp on high: thou hast led captiuitie captiue, and receiued giftes for men: yea, euen the rebellious hast thou led, that the Lord God might dwell there" (Psalm 68:18). She thus lives up to the quality Scudamore ascribes to her, "huge heroicke magnanimity" (III.xi.19), Arthur's virtue, and becomes, like Arthur and Redcrosse, a harrower of hell.

3. Conclusion

In the 1590 *Faerie Queene* the underworld figures forth as the "multi-stranded braid" mentioned in the Introduction. Hell is spiritual in the *ars moriendi* tradition, geographical in classical myth, theological in Christ's descent, and sociological in the analogy to prostitution. But since each variation on the underworld is also psychological, *Spenser's Underworld* comes to rest on similarity-in-difference. In each case, the underworld relates to a continuity of psychological truths (initiation-victory and qualified victory).

Even in victory a Spenserian knight is reminded of the potential for weakness. Redcrosse witnesses the Seven Deadly Sins, kneels before Lucifera, and is wounded by Sans Joy. Duessa's letter at the end of Book I may reflect not only the old law and the continuing efforts of falseness to overcome truth but also the inner temptation of self-censure and the power of guilt to drag one into despair, which do not necessarily cease with the maturity of holiness. Guyon faints after his walk through Mammon's Cave and is merely continent at the end of his journey toward temperance: even at the climax of the Legend of Temperance the knight remains vulnerable to false appearances. Prince Arthur receives a Christ-like wound in his right side even as he vanquishes a pagan knight. Likewise, Britomart's journey through the House of Busirane mingles strength and weakness, for it depicts much the same qualified sense of victory: the nick that she receives from Busirane reveals that she is still subject to the weakness signified by the nick that she receives from Gardante.

For Spenser, there is vulnerability in triumph, and conquering a quality that opposes chastity provides a paradoxical reminder of its continuing power to afflict virtue. If Redcrosse, Guyon, and Britomart share the initiation-victory dyad as well as the achievement of a qualified victory, then Britomart's journey is indeed a "like race," with the related underworld material contributing heightened sense of unity, symmetry, and closure to the 1590 *Faerie Queene*.

NOTES

This book uses Edwin Greenlaw's ten-volume *The Works of Edmund Spenser: A Variorum Edition* (Baltimore: Johns Hopkins University Press, 1932-36), and the *Geneva Bible: A Facsimile of the 1560 Edition* (Madison: University of Wisconsin Press, 1969). All references to these works appear in the text. I have omitted the italics in quotations from the *ars moriendi* literature and the Geneva Bible.

Introduction

1. A. C. Hamilton, "'Like Race To Runne': The Parallel Structure of *The Faerie Queene*, Books I and II," *PMLA* 73 (1958): 327-34; A. S. P. Woodhouse, "Nature and Grace in *The Faerie Queene*" (1949), in *Essential Articles for the Study of Edmund Spenser*, ed. A. C. Hamilton (Hamden, Conn.: Archon, 1972), 58-83; Thomas E. Maresca, *Three English Epics* (Lincoln: University of Nebraska Press, 1979), 24.

2. Ronald A. Horton, "Virtues," in *The Spenser Encyclopedia*, ed. A. C. Hamilton et al. (Toronto: University of Toronto Press, 1990), 720.

3. For the Church Fathers see J. A. MacCulloch, *The Harrowing of Hell: A Comparative Study of an Early Christian Doctrine* (Edinburgh: T. & T. Clark, 1930). Jackson J. Campbell deals with the Gospel of Nicodemus and the descent into hell in Old English poetry in "To Hell and Back: Latin Tradition and Literary Use of the 'Descensus ad Inferos' in Old English," *Viator: Medieval and Renaissance Studies* 13 (1982): 107-58. Spenser mentions the harrowing of hell in *The Faerie Queene* I.x.40, and in *Amoretti* 68.

4. Virgil, *Aeneid*, trans. Allen Mandelbaum (New York: Bantam, 1978). This material is quoted with the permission of Bantam Books, a division of Random House, Inc.

5. E. M. Burke, "Grace," *The New Catholic Encyclopedia* (New York: McGraw-Hill, 1967), 6:669-70.

6. Patrick Cullen, *The Infernal Triad: The Flesh, the World, and the Devil in Spenser and Milton* (Princeton: Princeton University Press, 1974), 89.

110

7. Perhaps the most explicit link between psychology and hell is Pyrochles's fury, which the poet describes in terms of hell fire at II.vi.44, 50.

8. John Calvin, *The Institutes of the Christian Religion*, trans. Ford Lewis Battles, ed. John T. McNeill (Philadelphia: Westminster, 1960), 3:60.

9. C. A. Patrides, "Renaissance and Modern Views on Hell," *Harvard Theological Review* 57 (1964): 217-36.

10. Ibid. This distinction runs throughout Patrides's article.

11. Judith H. Anderson, "Redcrosse and the Descent into Hell," *ELH* 36 (1969): 470-92.

12. Ibid., 480.

13. Frank Kermode's "The Cave of Mammon" was originally published in *Stratford-on-Avon Studies* 2 (1960): 151-74. The quotation is taken from the reprinted essay in Kermode's *Shakespeare, Spenser, Donne* (London: Routledge & Kegan Paul, 1971), 83. Other fine readings of Guyon's underworld journey include the following: Paul J. Alpers, "Interpreting the Cave of Mammon," Chapter 8 in *The Poetry of the Faerie Queene* (Princeton: Princeton University Press, 1967), 235-75; Harry Berger, Jr., *The Allegorical Temper: Vision and Reality in Book II of Spenser's Faerie Queene* (New Haven: Yale University Press, 1957); Patrick Cullen, "Guyon *Microchristus*," in *The Infernal Triad*, 68-96; and William M. McKim, Jr., "The Divine and Infernal Comedy of Spenser's Mammon," *Essays in Literature* 1 (1974): 3-16. Futher studies relevant to Mammon's Cave are cited in Chapters Three and Four.

14. Stephen Greenblatt, *Renaissance Self-Fashioning: From More to Shakespeare* (Chicago: University of Chicago Press, 1980), 179.

Chapter One

1. This chapter focuses on some of the texts anthologized in David William Atkinson's *The English* ars moriendi (New York: Peter Lang, 1992), hereafter referred to simply as "Atkinson." Specific titles appear below.

2. See *Variorum* 10:27-38. Harold L. Weatherby states in *The Spenser Encyclopedia* that "an English version (pub 1592) has been attributed to Spenser" (s.v. "*Axiochus*," 77).

3. James Nohrnberg's reference to "the death exhibiting a healthy

conscience, a calm mind and patient trust in one's author, and a resigning to Him of the ultimate issues of life and death" nicely summarizes the art of holy dying (*The Analogy of* The Faerie Queene [Princeton: Princeton University Press, 1976], 203). Two other critics, Kathrine Koller ("Art, Rhetoric, and Holy Dying in the *Faerie Queene* with Special Reference to the Despair Canto," *Studies in Philology* 61 [1964]: 128-39) and Bettie Anne Doebler (*Rooted Sorrow: Dying in Early Modern England* [Rutherford, N.J.: Fairleigh Dickinson University Press, 1994]) have both discussed the way in which the *ars moriendi* informs Spenser's Despaire episode. Koller shows that Spenser uses both rhetorical and pictorial elements of the literature of dying well. Despaire, of course, personifies one of the five deathbed temptations and, like the demons in the *ars moriendi* tradition, tries to get Redcrosse to think only of his slaughter, perjury, and fornication (ix.43, 46). He is even—as Koller does not mention—"a man of hell" (I.ix.28), tempting Redcrosse, as Ernest Sirluck notes ("A Note on the Rhetoric of Spenser's Despair," *Modern Philology* 47 [1949]: 8-11), to commit suicide by stressing justice and law and by omitting God's mercy and forgiveness. Then Despaire argues not only that death is the absence of sin and misery and the presence of rest and peace but also that, if Redcrosse dies now, his punishment in hell will be less. When these verbal arguments do not work, Despaire tries a pictorial strategy: he shows Redcrosse an image depicting the everlasting torment of human souls in hell. Their whole debate takes place in a setting where "Caves, owls, graves, ruined trees, dead men, [and] gibbets" all reinforce the certainty of physical death and eternal punishment (Koller, 135). Doebler mentions the dagger with which Redcrosse almost ends his life (105). All of these visual details clearly tie in with the pictorial dimension of the *ars moriendi* tradition. As Koller observes, Redcrosse's response, a feeble classical one, that he should do his duty, is not sufficient in his debate with Despaire (138), a failure, I would add, that illustrates Erasmus's sense that "with the deuyll we shoulde not dispute" (*Preparatione to Deathe*, in Atkinson, 61; this English translation appeared in 1538, four years after the Latin *De preparatione ad mortem*; the translator is not named). Insofar as Una, the personification of the true Church, reminds Redcrosse of God's merciful forgiveness and of the fact that he is one of the elect, she plays a positive role modeled on the angels, saints and good counselors in the *ars moriendi* tradition.

4. Psalm 91:11, for example, is cited in the *ars moriendi* literature: "For he shal giue his Angels charge ouer thee to kepe thee in all thy waies." The bedside psychomachia is much like the Good Angel's attempts to win the soul of Doctor Faustus in Marlowe's play.

5. Nancy Lee Beaty, *The Craft of Dying: A Study in the Literary Tradition of the* Ars Moriendi *in England*, Yale Studies in English, no. 175 (New Haven: Yale University Press, 1970), 12.

112

6. These contrasting positions are from Erasmus, *Preparatione to Deathe* (in Atkinson, 64), and William Caxton, *The Arte & Crafte to Know Well to Dye* (in Atkinson, 23). The latter, dated 1490, is Caxton's translation from the original French.

7. Qtd. in Susan Snyder, "The Left Hand of God: Despair in Medieval and Renaissance Tradition," *Studies in the Renaissance* 12 (1965), 21.

8. W. Harry Rylands, ed., *The Ars Moriendi (ca. 1450), A reproduction of the copy in the British Museum* (London: Holbein Society, 1881), n.p. Other exempla for combating despair include David, the prodigal son, Matthew, and the city of Nineveh (Snyder, "Left Hand of God," 26, 33). Cf. Charles A. Huttar, "Frail Grass and Firm Tree: David as a Model of Repentance in the Middle Ages and Early Renaissance," *The David Myth in Western Literature*, ed. Raymond-Jean Frontain and Jan Wojcik (West Lafayette, Ind.: Purdue University Press, 1980), 39, 190 n. 48.

9. Caxton, *Arte & Crafte*, in Atkinson, 13, 29. Erasmus, *Preparatione*, in Atkinson, 57. Cp. *Hamlet* I.v.78: "Unhouseled, disappointed, unaneled" (*The Complete Works of Shakespeare*, ed. David Bevington, 4th ed. [New York: HarperCollins, 1992]). William Perkins, *A Salve for a Sicke Man* (1595), in Atkinson, 144, 147.

10. Michael Schoenfeldt, *Bodies and Selves in Early Modern England: Physiology and Inwardness in Spenser, Shakespeare, Herbert, and Milton* (Cambridge: Cambridge University Press, 1999), 40.

11. Doebler, *Rooted Sorrow*, 104.

12. *Variorum* 1:233-34.

13. See *Purgatorio* 1.52-54.

14. *The Oxford English Dictionary*, 2nd ed. (1989), s.v. "spright" (def. 2). Charles Grosvenor Osgood also bears out this dual interpretation of "spright" with multiple examples of each sense of the word (*A Concordance to the Poems of Edmund Spenser*, Carnegie Institution of Washington Publications [Philadelphia: J. B. Lippincott, 1915], 809-10).

15. These include R. E. Neil Dodge, *The Complete Poetical Works of Edmund Spenser: Cambridge Edition* (Boston: Houghton Mifflin, 1908); Edwin Greenlaw, *Variorum*; and Thomas P. Roche, Jr., *The Faerie Queene* (New Haven:

Yale University Press, 1981).

16. J. C. Smith and E. de Selincourt, *The Poetical Works of Edmund Spenser* (London: Oxford University Press, 1932); P. C. Bayley, ed., *The Faerie Queene* (Oxford: Oxford University Press, 1966); Hugh Maclean, ed., *A Norton Critical Edition: Edmund Spenser's Poetry* (New York: Norton, 1968); and A. C. Hamilton, ed., *The Faerie Queene* (New York: Longman, 1977). For Hamilton's comments on glossing see "On Annotating Spenser's *Faerie Queene*: A New Approach to the Poem," in *Contemporary Thought on Edmund Spenser*, ed. Richard C. Frushell and Bernard J. Vondersmith (Carbondale: Southern Illinois University Press, 1975): 41-60.

17. Osgood, *Concordance*, 435-36, and *OED*, s.v. "ill" (B.1). For "ill" as sick, see A.8.a. The headnote to "ill" states: "Although *ill* is not etymologically related to *evil* the two words have from the 12th c. been synonymous, and *ill* has been often viewed as a mere variant or reduced form of *evil*."

18. William Shakespeare, *Hamlet*, ed. David Bevington, 4th ed. (New York: HarperCollins, 1992). See also Lawrence Babb, *The Elizabethan Malady: A Study of Melancholia in English Literature from 1580 to 1642* (East Lansing: Michigan State College Press, 1951), 108, 111, 49, 51. Cf. Burton, *Anatomy*, III, 393, 452-53.

19. For possible parallels in biblical language, see Naseeb Shaheen, *Biblical References in* The Faerie Queene (Memphis: Memphis State University Press, 1976).

20. Snyder, "Left Hand of God," 35.

21. Kerby Neill, "The Degradation of the Redcrosse Knight," *ELH* 19 (1952): 185. "This classic work on witchcraft went through six editions between 1576 and 1598 . . . and had an enormous authority in Spenser's lifetime. According to Joost Damhouder, sixteenth-century criminologist, it was equal to law . . . " (185, n. 21).

22. Babb, *Elizabethan Malady*, 110.

23. For Upton's full genealogy see *Variorum* 1:230.

24. "Physical debilitation, added to deep melancholy, naturally leads to a distaste for life. . . . The deranging effects of melancholy can thus account for suicide in a state of despair" (Snyder, "Left Hand of God," 53-54).

25. Caxton, *Arte & Crafte*, 48. Thomas Becon's Philemon states, "The manner of Sathan, which is the common aduersary of all men, is when any man is greuously sicke & like to dye, straightwayes to come vppon him at the begynning very fiercely, & to shew hymself terrible vnto him, & to caste before hys eyes such a myste that, except he taketh heede, he shall see nothing but the fierce wrath and terrible iudgemente of God agaynst sinners, agaynst sinne, desperation, death & hell, and whatsoeuer maketh vnto the better confusion of the sicke mans conscience" (*The Sicke Mans Salve* [1561], in Atkinson, 116). "When a man is most neere death, then the diuell is most busie in temptation, & the more men are assaulted by Satan, the more daungerous & troublesome is their case" (Perkins, *A Salve*, 132). To sum up, "the devil . . . works hardest in our death hour" (Sister Mary Catharine O'Connor, *The Art of Dying Well: The Development of the Ars Moriendi* [New York: AMS, 1966], 199). Philemon contradicts himself, though, when he claims that sickness is "to the body weaknesse and trouble, yet to the soule health and consolation" (Becon, 91).

26. For religious melancholy see Robert Burton, *The Anatomy of Melancholy*, ed. Floyd Dell & Paul Jordan-Smith (New York: Tudor 1938), 866-971, Sect. 4, Memb. 1, Sub. 1, and Memb. 2, Subs. 1.

27. A slightly different formulation appears in Snyder: "It is not the demon that causes sorrow . . . [as summarized by Chrysostom] but sorrow [that] directs one to the demon" ("Left Hand of God," 35).

28. Virgil K. Whitaker, *The Religious Basis of Spenser's Thought* (1950) (reprinted New York: Gordian, 1966), 44-45.

29. Atkinson, xii; and "The English Ars Morendi [*sic*]: Its Protestant Transformation," *Renaissance and Reformation* N.S. 6 (1982): 7-8. For the waning of the notion of hell in the seventeenth century see D. P. Walker, *The Decline of Hell: Seventeenth-Century Discussions of Eternal Torment* (Chicago: University of Chicago Press, 1964).

30. Doebler finds little "agreement about the mingling of Roman Catholic, Anglican, and Puritan elements" in the Despaire episode. "Literature," she continues, "often softens theological distinctions as it focuses upon the ambiguities of experience" (*Rooted Sorrow*, 27).

31. John N. King, *Spenser's Poetry and the Reformation Tradition* (Princeton: Princeton University Press, 1990), 9-10; and Carol Kaske, *Spenser and Biblical Poetics* (Ithaca: Cornell University Press, 1999), 4.

32. John F. H. New, *Anglican and Puritan: The Basis of Their*

Opposition, 1558-1640 (Stanford, Calif.: Stanford University Press, 1964), 81.

33. Kaske, *Spenser and Biblical Poetics*, 101.

34. Snyder, "Left Hand of God," 40, 26. See also E. J. Bicknell, *A Theological Introduction to the Thirty-Nine Articles of the Church of England*, 3d ed., revised by H. J. Carpenter (London: Longmans, 1963), 227.

35. Darryl J. Gless, *Interpretation and Theology in Spenser* (Cambridge: Cambridge University Press, 1994), 14. Gless discusses the Despaire canto on pages 143-45. Walker's statement about predestination is also relevant here: "He [God] gives commands to men whom, by His eternal decree of reprobation, He forces to disobey, and also, by the preaching of the Gospel, offers them salvation from which He has already decided to exclude them" (*Decline of Hell*, 49). Cf. *The Thirty-Nine Articles of Religion*, available at the following website: http://web.singnet.com/sg/~kohfly/articles.html.

36. Kaske, *Spenser and Biblical Poetics*, 101.

37. New, *Anglican and Puritan*, 77.

38. John Pearson, *An Exposition of the Creed* (1659), 8th ed. (London: n.p., 1704), 394.

39. Thomas Lupset, *The Waye of Dyenge Well* (1538), in Atkinson, 86.

40. Perkins, *A Salve*, in Atkinson, 141.

41. Beaty, *The Craft of Dying*, 27.

42. Whitaker, *Religious Basis*, 46, 44; James Schiavoni, "Predestination and Free Will: The Crux of Canto 10," *Spenser Studies* 10 (1992): 175-95; and Robert L. Reid, "Holiness, house of," in *The Spenser Encyclopedia*, 374. Charles E. Mounts demonstrates that Spenser's beadsmen come from Lactantius through Bullinger, a reformer. Thus their presence in Canto 10 may demonstrate a mixture of Catholic and Protestant traditions ("Spenser's Seven Bead-men and the Corporal Works of Mercy," *PMLA* 54 [1939]: 974-80).

43. Caxton, *Arte & Crafte*, in Atkinson, 20.

44. Becon, *The Sicke Mans Salve*, in Atkinson, 114.

45. For a contrasting view see Harold Skulsky, "Spenser's Despair

116

Episode and the Theology of Doubt," *Modern Philology* 78 (1981): 234. "It is hard to avoid the conclusion that in her rebuttal to Despair Una has succeeded in showing Redcrosse only (as we anticipated) that he has been given no ground for thinking he is damned, but that at the same time she has failed in what I shall now argue is her peculiar mission to give him, by her very presence, a ground for thinking he is Elect—indeed, a ground that cannot be false. Now it is true, as the sequel shows, that Redcrosse is Elect all the same. His belief is *true*, then; it is *justified* (in a degree) by Una's testimony. But it is not the kind of cognition that the Reformers call *fiducia*—not quite the *evidence* of things unseen . . . we have a justified true belief that stops just short of being knowledge."

46. David Lee Cressy, *Birth, Marriage, and Death: Ritual, Religion, and the Life-Cycle in Tudor and Stuart England* (New York: Oxford University Press, 1997), 392.

47. For the controversy on sainthood in this life versus the next, see Schiavoni, "Predestination and Free Will," 181-82; and Anthea Hume, *Edmund Spenser: Protestant Poet* (Cambridge: Cambridge University Press, 1984), 70-71.

48. Carol Zaleski, *Otherworld Journeys: Accounts of Near-Death Experience in Medieval and Modern Times* (New York: Oxford University Press, 1987), 77.

49. Beaty, *The Craft of Dying*, 112.

50. Eric R. Seeman, "'She Died Like Good Old Jacob': Deathbed Scenes and Inversions of Power in New England, 1675-1775," *Proceedings of the American Antiquarian Society* 104 (1994): 286-87.

51. Kaske, *Spenser and Biblical Poetics*, 156; and Gless, *Interpretation and Theology in Spenser*, 147.

52. *The Booke of the Craft of Dying*, qtd. in Zaleski, *Otherworld Journeys*, 50.

53. A. C. Hamilton, "'Like Race To Runne': The Parallel Structure of *The Faerie Queene*, Books I and II," *PMLA* 73 (1958): 332.

54. John Erskine Hankins, *Source and Meaning in Spenser's Allegory: A Study of 'The Faerie Queene'* (Oxford: Oxford University Press, 1971), 44.

55. Becon, *The Sicke Mans Salve*, in Atkinson, 107. For "race" see also I

Corinthians 9:24, Galatians 5:7, and 2 Timothy 4:7.

56. *OED*, s.v. "race" (I.1.c).

57. Cicero, qtd. in Koller, "Art, Rhetoric, and Holy Dying," 31.

Chapter Two

1. For a general study of Theseus in the Renaissance, see D'Orsay W. Pearson, "'Unkinde' Theseus: A Study in Renaissance Mythography," *English Literary Renaissance* 4 (1974): 276-98. Cf. Richard L. Hoffman, "Ovid and Chaucer's Myth of Theseus and Pirithous," *English Language Notes* 2 (1965): 252-57; and Henry J. Webb, "A Reinterpretation of Chaucer's Theseus," *Review of English Studies* 23 (1947): 289-96. For a concise summary of the life of Theseus, see Ruth B. Edwards, "The Story of Theseus," in *The Quest for Theseus*, ed. Anne G. Ward et al. (New York: Praeger Publishers, 1970), 7-27. For an account of Spenser's use of the Theseus legend in *The Faerie Queene* see D'Orsay W. Pearson, "Theseus, Hippolytus," in *The Spenser Encyclopedia*, ed. A. C. Hamilton et al. (Toronto: University of Toronto Press, 1990), 686-87. For commentary on Theseus in Book VI see Donald Cheney, *Spenser's Image of Nature: Wild Man and Shepherd in "The Faerie Queene"* (New Haven: Yale University Press, 1966), 227-38.

2. Plutarch, "The Life of Theseus," in *The Lives*, trans. Sir Thomas North (New York: AMS Press, 1967; reprint of 1579 ed.), 1:59.

3. Spenser's source for this line is Boccaccio's *Genealogia* I.14: "*Theseum perpetuo damnatum otio.*"

4. On Spenser and classical myth see the following: Thomas F. Bulger, "Classical Vision and Christian Revelation: Spenser's Use of Mythology in Book I of *The Faerie Queene*," *Greyfriar* 23 (1982): 5-25; Douglas Bush, *Mythology and the Renaissance Tradition in English Poetry* (Minneapolis: University of Minnesota Press, 1932) and *Pagan Myth and Christian Tradition in English Poetry* (Philadelphia: American Philosophical Society, 1968), esp. 11, n. 17; Angus Fletcher, *The Prophetic Moment: An Essay on Spenser* (Chicago: University of Chicago Press, 1971), 76-106; A. C. Hamilton, "Spenser's Treatment of Myth," *ELH* 26 (1959): 335-54; Merritt Y. Hughes, *Virgil and Spenser* (Berkeley: University of California Press, 1929); Theresa M. Krier, *Gazing on Secret Sights: Spenser, Classical Imitation, and the Decorums of Vision* (Ithaca: Cornell University Press, 1990); C. W. Lemmi, "The Symbolism of the Classical Episodes in *The Faerie Queene*," *Philological Quarterly* 8 (1929): 270-87; Henry Gibbons Lotspeich, *Classical Mythology in the Poetry of Edmund*

Spenser (Princeton: Princeton University Press, 1932); James Nohrnberg, *The Analogy of* The Faerie Queene (Princeton: Princeton University Press, 1976); William A. Sessions, "Spenser's Georgics," *English Literary Renaissance* 10 (1980): 202-38; and W. S. Webb, "Vergil in Spenser's Epic Theory," in *Critical Essays on Spenser from ELH* (Baltimore: n.p., 1970), 1-23. For Spenser's main classical sources see Natalis Comes, *Mythologiae* (New York: Garland Publishing, 1976); and *Shakespeare's Ovid: Being Arthur Golding's Translation of the "Metamorphoses"*, ed. W. H. D. Rouse (Carbondale: Southern Illinois University Press, 1961).

5. These two types are closely analogous to what William Blissett calls the "center-seeking labyrinth" and the "transit maze," respectively ("Caves, Labyrinths, and *The Faerie Queene*," in *Unfolded Tales: Essays on Renaissance Romance*, ed. George Logan and Gordon Teskey [Ithaca: Cornell University Press, 1989], 286-87). Angus Fletcher calls the multicursal labyrinth simply an *"intricate system of paths"* ("The Image of Lost Direction," in *Centre and Labyrinth: Essays in Honour of Northrop Frye*, ed. Eleanor Cook et al. [Toronto: University of Tornoto Press, 1983], 334). For general studies of the labyrinth see Janet Bord, *Mazes and Labyrinths of the World* (New York: E. P. Dutton, 1975); Rodney Castledon, *The Knossos Labyrinth: A New View of the "Palace of Minos" at Knossos* (London: Routledge, 1990); Penelope Reed Doob, *The Idea of the Labyrinth from Classical Antiquity through the Middle Ages* (Ithaca: Cornell University Press, 1990); W. F. Jackson Knight, *Vergil: Epic and Anthropology* (New York: Barnes & Noble, 1967); and W. H. Matthews, *Mazes and Labyrinths: Their History and Development* (New York: Dover, 1970).

6. Fletcher, ibid.; and Blissett, "Caves, Labyrinths," in *Unfolded Tales*, 287.

7. Doob, *Idea of the Labyrinth*, 62n.

8. The *OED* defines *labyrinth* as "a structure consisting of a number of intercommunicating passages arranged in bewildering complexity, through which it is difficult or impossible to find one's way without guidance; a maze" (def. 1). A *maze* is "a structure consisting of a network of winding and intercommunicating paths and passages arranged in bewildering complexity, so that without guidance it is difficult to find one's way in it; a labyrinth; *occas.* in *plural*, the windings of a labyrinth" (4.a). For "maze" as a noun with psychological implications, see 1.a and 3.a.

9. Knight, *Vergil*, 248.

10. Ibid., 247.

11. Matthews, *Mazes and Labyrinths*, 23. He points out, however, that "discoveries of recent years have considerably diminished [the Gortyna Cavern's] claim to be considered as the original Labyrinth of the Minotaur" (28). Castledon in *The Knossos Labyrinth* concludes that the palace of Minos at Knossos is the original labyrinth.

12. Knight, *Vergil*, 218.

13. James Nohrnberg makes the basic analogy this way: "At her separation from Redcrosse, Una reminds us of an abandoned Ariadne: her knight defeats the monster in the labyrinth; for mysterious reasons she is thereafter forsaken (sometimes in connection with a dream or spell from Bacchus); and she laments that the beasts are kinder than her lover" (*Analogy*, 271).

14. Doob, *Idea of the Labyrinth*, 126, 151.

15. The point appears in Angus Fletcher's discussion of Hawthorne's "The Minotaur." "In effect," he writes, "the cord becomes an extrusion of Ariadne's hand and implies that, with it in hand, the hero suffers no discontinuity with the outside of the maze. He never, in effect, leaves the outside" ("Image of Lost Direction," 337). D'Orsay W. Pearson refers to the thread as reason ("Spenser's Labyrinth—Again," *Studies in Iconography* 3 [1977]: 80).

16. Qtd. in Bord, *Mazes and Labyrinths*, 88.

17. Cheney, *Spenser's Image of Nature*, 233.

18. Pearson, "Spenser's Labyrinth," 76; *Ovide Moralisé*, ed. C. De Boer et al., vol. 3 (Amsterdam: Uitgave van de N. V. Noord-Hollandsche Uitgeversmaatschappij, 1931), 8:1565-70.

19. H. S. V. Jones, *A Spenser Handbook* (New York: F. S. Crofts, 1930), 159.

20. Bulger, "Classical Vision," 15.

21. Cicero, qtd. in Plutarch, *Lives*, 1:41.

22. Lillian Feder, *Ancient Myth in Modern Poetry* (Princeton: Princeton University Press, 1971), 35, 373.

23. In terms of eros, the battles against the Minotaur and Errour are

appropriately set: in Spenser's day the Cretan Labyrinth, like the Minotaur, represented the unrestrained sensuality opposing progress by reason or the spirit. Charles A. Huttar states more generally: "It is not accidental that caves and labyrinths have a sexual symbolism and that finding one's way in a maze is an initiation suitable to coming-of-age" ("Hell and the City: Tolkien and the Traditions of Western Literature," *A Tolkien Compass*, ed. Jared Lobdell [La Salle, Ill.: Open Court, 1975], 125). This view of the labyrinth as an emblem of sensuality is wholly more sensible than Freud's reading of the image. "As an example [of dreams' elucidation of mythological themes]," writes Feder, "he [Freud] suggests that 'the Labyrinth can be recognized as a representation of anal birth: the twisting paths are the bowels and Ariadne's thread is the umbilical cord'" (*Ancient Myth*, 37-38). See Sigmund Freud, "Revision of the Theory of Dreams," in *The Standard Edition of the Complete Psychological Works*, ed. and trans. James Strachey (London: Hogarth Press, 1964), 22:25.

24. Freud, "The Acquisition and Control of Fire," *Standard Edition*, 22:189.

25. Doob, *Idea of the Labyrinth*, 9.

26. Plutarch, *Lives*, 41.

27. Knight, *Vergil*, 250.

28. Ibid., 192-93.

29. See Matthew 7:13: "Enter in at the streicte gate for it is the wide gate, and broad waye that leadeth to destruction and manie there be which go in thereat."

30. Judith H. Anderson, "Redcrosse and the Descent into Hell," *ELH* 36 (1969): 485ff.; and *The Growth of a Personal Voice: "Piers Plowman" and "The Faerie Queene"* (New Haven: Yale University Press, 1976), 37-40.

31. Regarding the Hippolytus story, Lotspeich writes, "Bocc. [10.50] here supplies all the material of Spenser's version in Spenser's order, except two details: that Phaedra killed herself with a knife, and that Theseus, with Diana's help, gathered up Hippolytus's remains. Both of these points seem to be peculiar to Spenser, but for the latter he may have received a suggestion from *Aen.* 7.765-769" (*Classical Mythology*, 70). Bulger also identifies Spenser's alteration of the Aesculapius myth but not its parallel to Theseus's eternal damnation ("Classical Visions," 21).

32. Matthews, *Mazes and Labyrinths*, 34-35.

33. Doob, *Idea of the Labyrinth*, 56. Fletcher calls this disorientation "mental bafflement" and states that the labyrinth is a *"metaphor* for any inextricably difficult situation where the very structure of the difficulty cannot be discerned" ("The Image of Lost Direction," 330, 334). Using Frye's phrase, Blissett refers to the "loss of a sense of direction" ("Caves, Labyrinths," in *Unfolded Tales*, 288). An excellent statement on the same principle comes from Jungian analyst Joseph L. Henderson: "The experience of the labyrinth, whether as a pictorial design, a dance, a garden path or a system of corridors in a temple, always has the same psychological effect. It temporarily disturbs rational conscious orientation to the point that . . . the initiate is 'confused' and symbolically 'loses his way'" (Joseph L. Henderson and Maud Oakes, *The Wisdom of the Serpent* [New York: George Braziller, 1963], qtd. in Bord, *Mazes and Labyrinths*, 103). Disorientation is precisely what Redcrosse and his companions experience in Canto 1, stanza 10.

34. Doob, *Idea of the Labyrinth*, 56.

35. Ronald A. Horton, "Dwarfs," in *The Spenser Encyclopedia*, 230.

36. Virgil, *Aeneid*, trans. Allen Mandelbaum (New York: Bantam Books, 1971). This material is quoted with the permission of Bantam Books, a division of Random House, Inc.

37. Doob, *Idea of the Labyrinth*, 238-39.

38. Knight, *Vergil*, 267.

39. Ibid., 11. For critical interpretations of Virgil's maze, see also Knight's "Vergil and the Maze," *Classical Review* 43 (1929): 212-13; *Cumean Gates* (Oxford: Blackwell, 1936), Chapter 9; and *Roman Vergil* (London: Faber and Faber, 1944), 166; Brooks Otis, *Vergil: A Study in Civilized Poetry* (Oxford: Clarendon Press, 1963), 284-85; C. J. Putnam, *The Poetry of the Aeneid* (Cambridge, Mass.: Harvard University Press, 1965), Chapter 2, esp. 92-99; and Colin Still, *The Timeless Theme* (London: Nicholson & Watson, 1936), 99-100. For a summary of Servius's view of the forests through which Aeneas passes, see J. W. Jones, "Allegorical Interpretations in Servius," *Classical Journal* 56 (1961): 217-26.

40. Jung comments on "the fate of Theseus and Peirithous, who descended into Hades and grew fast to the rocks of the underworld, which is to say that the conscious mind, advancing into the unknown regions of the psyche, is

overpowered by the archaic forces of the unconscious." See "The Prima Materia," in *The Collected Works*, vol. 12, ed. Herbert Read et al., trans. R. F. C. Hull (London: Routledge & Kegan Paul, 1953), par. 438.

41. Edwards, "Story of Theseus," 20-23. The *Aeneid* is Spenser's source for Theseus's eternal presence in hell. Other sources stress the classical hero's absence from the underworld. For example, in Statius's *Thebaid* Erebus laments that Theseus is not in hell (VIII.51-57), and in the *Inferno* the furies complain that they let Theseus go too easily (IX.54). A definitive comment by Nohrnberg shows that the Theseus myth animated Spenser's imagination in Book II as well: "Mammon's stool is in the underworld, and there is only one such seat in the classical Hades, that being the one to which Theseus was anchored" (*Analogy*, 342).

42. John W. Zarker, "Aeneas and Theseus in *Aeneid* 6," *Classical Journal* 62 (1976): 225. For the critical debate on Theseus as the speaker of this warning, see Zarker's note 22.

43. Frank Kermode comments on Theseus's damnation: "Theseus was condemned *to* sloth, not *for* sloth; in fact he had just been attempting with some vigour the rape of Proserpina" ("The Cave of Mammon," *Stratford-on-Avon Studies* 2 [1960]: 164). The essay is reprinted in Kermode's *Shakespeare, Spenser, Donne* (London: Routledge & Kegan Paul, 1971), 60-83.

44. Bulger identifies Spenser's alteration of the Aesculapius myth but not its parallel to the eternal damnation of Theseus ("Classical Vision," 21).

45. Plutarch, *Lives*, 1:33.

46. Ibid., 33-34.

47. Ibid., 38.

48. These remarks on Theseus and strict justice are much in the spirit of Webb's study of Chaucer's Theseus in the *Knight's Tale* ("A Reinterpretation").

49. Doob, *Idea of the Labyrinth*, 1.

50. Ibid., 38.

51. "Thus," writes Fletcher, "when imprisoned there by Minos, he adds a knowing third dimension, and flies out. What he gets, by adding the third dimension, is perspective *on*, to replace direction *in*. With every added dimension

of perception of the maze, there will be an increase of power over the system of perilous convolutions. These perspectival distancings are mechanisms for achieving what direction alone must always lack, namely orientation" ("The Image of Lost Direction," 339). Fletcher does not relate the point to Redcrosse's vision.

52. Pearson, "Spenser's Labyrinth," 84.

53. Doob, *Idea of the Labyrinth*, 56.

54. For articulation of this point about other classical allusions see Bulger, "Classical Vision," 5-6, 10; Hamilton, "Spenser's Treatment of Myth," 335, 338; Pearson, "Spenser's Labyrinth," 71; and A. S. P. Woodhouse, "Nature and Grace in *The Faerie Queene*" (1949), in *Essential Articles for the Study of Edmund Spenser*, ed. A. C. Hamilton (Hamden, Conn.: Archon, 1972), 68.

Chapter Three

1. Penelope Reed Doob, *The Idea of the Labyrinth from Classical Antiquity through the Middle Ages* (Ithaca: Cornell University Press, 1990), 126, 151.

2. Harold L. Weatherby, *Mirrors of Celestial Grace: Patristic Theology in Spenser's Allegory* (Toronto: University of Toronto Press, 1994), 134-37.

3. Anthea Hume, *Edmund Spenser: Protestant Poet* (Cambridge: Cambridge University Press, 1984), 63.

4. E. M. Burke, "Grace," *The New Catholic Encyclopedia* (New York: McGraw-Hill, 1967), 6:669-70; and "Grace," in *The Oxford Dictionary of the Christian Church*, ed. F. L. Cross and E. A. Livingstone (London: Oxford University Press, 1974), 586-87.

5. John Calvin, *The Institutes of the Christian Religion*, ed. John T. McNeill, trans. Ford Lewis Battles (Philadelphia: Westminster, 1960), 1:48.

6. Weatherby, *Mirrors*, 11.

7. The only biblical passage that specifically refers to Christ's descent into hell is I Peter 3:18-20: Christ "went, & preached unto the spirits that were in prison." Matthew 12:40 regarding Jonah in the belly of the whale was also thought to suggest the descent. Numerous other passages suggest the descent less directly: Judges 16:30, Isaiah 42:7, Daniel 3:25, Zechariah 9:11, and Luke 11:21-22. Besides the primary sources cited in the text, one may wish to consult

Thomas Bilson, *The effect of certaine Sermons Tovching the Fvll Redemption of mankind by the death and bloud of Christ Jesus* (London: Peter Short, 1599), 219-20. A useful secondary source is Dewey D. Wallace, Jr., "Puritan and Anglican: The Interpretation of Christ's Descent Into Hell and Elizabethan Theology," *Archive for Reformation History* 69 (1978): 248-87.

8. Adam Hill, *The Defence of the Article: Christ Descended into Hell* (London: n.p., 1592), 20. Although the 1590 edition of *The Faerie Queene* predates this text, I regard Hill's comment as representative of a debate that had gone on well before Spenser wrote Books I and II. For an overview of this debate, see Peter Milward, *Religious Controversies of the Elizabethan Age: A Survey of Printed Sources* (Lincoln: University of Nebraska Press, 1977), 163-68.

9. Thomas Becon, "The Sick Man's Salve," folio ed. 1561, in *Prayers and Other Pieces of Thomas Becon*, ed. John Ayre, Parker Society No. 4 (Cambridge: Cambridge University Press, 1844), 139.

10. Thomas Cranmer, "Corrections of the Institution of a Christian Man, by Henry VIII. With Archbishop Cranmer's Annotations" (1538), in *Miscellaneous Writings and Letters of Thomas Cranmer*, ed. John Edmund Cox, Parker Society No. 16 (Cambridge: Cambridge University Press, 1846), 89. It is not clear from Cranmer's annotation on this passage whether he thinks that Christ went to hell only in his human soul or in his godhead as well: "And I believe assuredly that this our Saviour Jesu Christ, after he was thus crucified, dead upon the cross, and buried, descended with his soul into hell, leaving his blessed body in sepulture here in earth, and loosed the pains and sorrows thereof, where with it was not possible that he should be holden."

11. John Longland, *A Sermond [sic] spoken before the kynge his maiestie at Grenwiche, vppon good fryday: the yere of our Lord 1536* (London: T. Petyt, 1538).

12. *Here Begynneth the Treatys of Nicodemus Gospel* (n.p., 1532), n.p. A useful modern edition is *The Middle-English Harrowing of Hell and Gospel of Nicodemus*, ed. William Henry Hulme (London: Oxford University Press, 1961). J. F. Goodridge, ed., *Piers the Ploughman*, by William Langland (Baltimore: Penguin, 1959), 40, 47; Langland (same edition), 253; Goodridge's note, in Langland, 357n.; "The Harrowing of Hell," in *The Exeter Book*, part 2, ed. W. S. Mackie, Early English Text Society No. 194 (London: Oxford University Press, 1934), line 41. The poem is almost entirely spoken by the soul of John the Baptist. As he preached Christ's incarnation, so he predicts Christ's coming to hell. Thomas Becon, *The Catechism of Thomas Becon, With Other Pieces Written by Him in the Reign of King Edward the Sixth*, ed. John Ayre, Parker Society No. 3

(Cambridge: Cambridge University Press, 1844), 33. Cf. Calvin, *Institutes,* 1:517.

13. A. S. P. Woodhouse, "Nature and Grace in *The Faerie Queene*" (1949), in *Essential Articles for the Study of Edmund Spenser*, ed. A.C. Hamilton (Hamden, Conn.: Archon, 1972), 65.

14. Hume, *Edmund Spenser*, 90.

15. For the image of brass doors, see J. A. MacCulloch, *The Harrowing of Hell: A Comparative Study of an Early Christian Doctrine* (Edinburgh: T. & T. Clark, 1930), 219.

16. Woodhouse writes, "When he [Arthur] intervenes to rescue Sir Guyon from the stealthy attack of Pyrochles and Cymochles, it is no longer as the symbol of heavenly grace intervening to save from inward evil, but as the symbol of magnanimity, swift to recognize a kindred spirit and to protect him from the outward depredation of his foes" ("Nature and Grace," 70). (I agree that Arthur's collective virtue is magnanimity, not the divine grace associated with him in Book I.) James Nohrnberg states, "At just this point Guyon's guardian spirit descends to take over for the senseless knight; the guardian's office in turn passes to Arthur, that is, to a 'self' who relies upon more than one virtue" (*The Analogy of The Faerie Queene* [Princeton: Princeton University Press, 1976], 351). And Gordon Teskey suggests: "According to Spenser's stated intentions in the Letter, Arthur is to represent not divine grace but that perfection of human nature which unites all virtues in itself. Left on its own, this ideal would suggest a Pelagian self-sufficiency, to which grace would be unnecessary. That is why the angel watches over Guyon before Arthur arrives: *not to identify Arthur with grace but to qualify his moral perfection as still being in need of divine aid*" (my emphasis; "Arthur in *The Faerie Queene*," in *The Spenser Encyclopedia*, ed. A. C. Hamilton et al. [Toronto: University of Toronto Press, 1990], 71).

17. Cf. John E. Hankins's helpful note in *The Spenser Encyclopedia*, s.v. "Psychomachia," 570. My reading is in harmony with his sense that Spenser's "figures may be read against many operative schemes such as Aristotelian psychology, Protestant doctrine, Platonic psychology, and contemporary English history."

18. The faint has been widely interpreted. Harry Berger, Jr., mentions three possible interpretations: it proves Guyon's excellence; it is irrelevant to his excellence; and "the faint questions and tests his excellence and proceeds perhaps from a peculiar limitation attendant on that excellence" (*The Allegorical Temper: Vision and Reality in Book II of Spenser's Faerie Queene* [New Haven: Yale

University Press, 1957], 16). Ernest Sirluck states, "Nothing in the canto suggests desire, and the collapse is explicitly and at length ascribed to purely physical causes (55-56)" ("The *Faerie Queene*, Book II, and the *Nicomachean Ethics*," *Modern Philology* 49 [1951]: 91). For Maurice Evans, "Guyon's faint clearly symbolizes the Fall of Adam" ("The Fall of Guyon," *ELH* 28 [1961]: 220). Patrick Cullen agrees that the faint is "the inevitable culmination of the Adamic weakness he has manifested throughout the ordeal. Accordingly, the image of Guyon prostrate on the earth is an image of man's bondage to the flesh, to the old Adam within who is 'of the earth, earthlie' (I Corinthians 15:47)" (*The Infernal Triad: The Flesh, the World, and the Devil in Spenser and Milton* [Princeton: Princeton University Press, 1974], 89). William M. McKim, Jr., states, "Thus his fainting at the end of the episode does not demonstrate a moral weakness peculiar to him but is a symbolic act, revealing the limitation of human reason in overcoming the consequences of original sin. His physical collapse, an image of death, unites him with a higher kind of grace than that of bountiful nature, a mystery of which he, as the embodiment of classical virtue, can be only imperfectly aware" ("The Divine and Infernal Comedy of Spenser's Mammon," *Essays in Literature* 1 [1974]: 12-13). A. C. Hamilton states that "the full limitation of natural virtue is seen when Guyon falls, and Arthur must come to rescue him. For though the temperate body is strong, being continually besieged, it stands only by the power of grace" (*The Structure of Allegory in "The Faerie Queene"* [Oxford: Clarendon Press, 1961], 101).

19. Calvin, *Institutes*, 1:765.

20. Weatherby, *Mirrors*, 137.

Chapter Four

1. A. C. Hamilton, "'Like Race To Runne': The Parallel Structure of *The Faerie Queene*, Books I and II," *PMLA* 73 (1958): 327-34.

2. René Graziani, "*The Faerie Queene*, Book II," in *The Spenser Encyclopedia*, ed. A. C. Hamilton et al. (Toronto: University of Toronto Press, 1990), 267.

3. Benjamin G. Lockerd, Jr., *The Sacred Marriage: Psychic Integration in "The Faerie Queene"* (London: Associated University Presses, 1987), 136.

4. Douglas Waters, *Duessa As Theological Satire* (Columbia: University of Missouri Press, 1970).

5. E. J. Burford, *Bawds and Lodgings: A History of the London Bankside*

Brothels c. 100-1675 (London: Peter Owen, 1976), 145.

6. John L. McMullan, *The Canting Crew: London's Criminal Underworld 1550-1700* (New Brunswick, N.J.: Rutgers University Press, 1984), 117.

7. Ian W. Archer, *The Pursuit of Stability: Social Relations in Elizabethan London* (Cambridge: Cambridge University Press, 1991), 215.

8. Qtd. in Amanda Anderson, "Prostitution's Artful Guise," review of Charles Bernheimer's *Figures of Ill Repute: Representing Prostitution in Nineteenth-Century France*, in *Diacritics: A Review of Contemporary Criticism* 21 (1991): 110.

9. Paul Griffiths, "The Structure of Prostitution in Elizabethan London," *Continuity and Change* 8 (1993): 50.

10. Kevin P. Siena, "Pollution, Promiscuity, and the Pox: English Venereology and the Early Modern Medical Discourse on Social and Sexual Danger," *Journal of the History of Sexuality* 8 (1998): 566.

11. Anne M. Haselkorn, *Prostitution in Elizabethan and Jacobean Comedy* (Troy, N.Y.: Whitston, 1983), 15.

12. Burford, *Bawds and Lodgings*, 145.

13. Michael Strachan, *The Life and Adventures of Thomas Coryate* (London: Oxford University Press, 1962), 40. I follow Strachan's conventions for the spelling of Thomas Coryate and *Coryat's Crudities*.

14. Manfred Pfister, "*The Passion* from Winterson to Coryate," in *Venetian Views, Venetian Blinds: English Fantasies of Venice*, ed. Manfred Pfister and Barbara Schaff (Amsterdam: Rodopi, 1999), 21-22.

15. Northrop Frye, *The Educated Imagination* (Bloomington: Indiana University Press, 1964), 63-64.

16. Brenda M. Hosington, "Idle Lake," in *The Spenser Encyclopedia*, 387.

17. John Dixon Hunt and Michael Leslie, "Gardens," in *The Spenser Encyclopedia*, 324.

18. Thomas Coryate, *Coryat's Crudities* (1611) (Glasgow: Robert

Maclehose, 1905), 404-406.

19. Ibid., 401-402.

20. Strachan, *Life of Coryate*, 50.

21. Coryate, *Crudities*, 408-409.

22. John Milton, *Areopagitica*, in *Complete Prose Works of John Milton*, ed. Ernest Sirluck et al. (New Haven: Yale University Press, 1959), 2:516.

23. Ibid., 2:515.

24. Ernest Sirluck, "The *Faerie Queene*, Book II, and the *Nicomachean Ethics*," *Modern Philology* 49 (1951): 78.

25. Coryate, *Crudities*, 404.

26. Sigmund Freud, "Totem and Taboo," in *The Standard Edition of the Complete Psychological Works*, ed. James Strachey (London: Hogarth Press, 1966), 13:29-32.

27. Ibid., 11:171.

28. Ibid., 13:30-31.

29. Coryate, *Crudities*, 405.

30. David G. Myers, *Social Psychology*, 7th ed. (New York: McGraw-Hill, 2002), 221.

31. Sirluck, "The *Faerie Queene*, Book II," 85, 90.

32. Lewis H. Miller, Jr., "Phaedria, Mammon, and Sir Guyon's Education by Error," *Journal of English and Germanic Philology* 63 (1964): 33.

33. Sirluck, "The *Faerie Queene*, Book II," 88.

34. Ibid., 85.

35. Ibid., 86.

36. Miller, "Phaedria," 37.

37. Augustine, *Confessions*, trans. J. G. Pilkington, in *Nicene and Post-Nicene Fathers*, vol. 1, ed. Philip Schaff (Peabody, Mass.: Hendrickson Publishers, 1995), 10:35. Harry Berger, Jr., quotes a slightly better translation: "Curiosity for trial's sake, seeketh even the contraries of these, not for the sake of suffering annoyances, but out of the lust of experiment and knowledge" (*The Allegorical Temper: Vision and Reality in Book II of Spenser's Faerie Queene* [New Haven: Yale University Press, 1957], 26).

38. Martha Carlin, *Medieval Southwark* (London: Hambledon, 1996), 347.

39. Charles Winick and Paul M. Kinsie, *The Lively Commerce: Prostitution in the United States* (Chicago: Quadrangle, 1971), 193.

40. On prostitution in medieval London, see Carlin, *Medieval Southwark*; E. Beresford Chancellor, *The Pleasure Haunts of London During Four Centuries* (Boston: Houghton Mifflin, 1925); David J. Johnson, *Southwark and the City* (London: Oxford University Press, 1969); Ruth Mazo Karras, *Common Women: Prostitution and Sexuality in Medieval England* (New York: Oxford University Press, 1996), and "Sex, Money, and Prostitution in Medieval English Culture," in *Desire and Discipline: Sex and Sexuality in the Premodern West*, ed. Jacqueline Murray and Konrad Eisenbichler (Toronto: University of Toronto Press, 1996), 201-16; Henry Ansgar Kelly, "Bishops, Prioress, and Bawd in the Stews of Southwark," *Speculum* 75 (2000): 342-88; William Rendle, "The Stews on Bankside," *Antiquarian Magazine & Bibliographer* 2 (1882): 70-77; G. T. Salisbury-Jones, *Street Life in Medieval England* (Totowa, N.J.: Rowman and Littlefield, 1975); and John Stow, *A Survey of London*, ed. Henry Morley (Dover, N.H.: Sutton, 1994).

On prostitution in sixteenth- and seventeenth-century London, see in addition to Stow's *Survey*: Caroline S. Andre, "Some Selected Aspects of the Role of Women in Sixteenth Century England," *International Journal of Women's Studies* 4 (1981): 76-88; Archer, *The Pursuit of Stability*; Normand Berlin, *The Base String: The Underworld in Elizabethan Drama* (Rutherford, N.J.: Fairleigh Dickinson University Press, 1968); Griffiths, "Structure of Prostitution"; Tim Harris, "The Bawdy House Riots of 1668," *Historical Journal* 29 (1986): 537-56; Haselkorn, *Prostitution*; A. V. Judges, *The Elizabethan Underworld* (London: George Routledge, 1930); Joseph Lenz, "Base Trade: Theater as Prostitution," *ELH* 60 (1993): 833-56; K. J. Lindley, "Riot Prevention and Control in Early Stuart London," *Transactions of the Royal Historical Society* 33 (1983): 109-26; John L. McMullan, *Canting Crew*; Gämini Salgädo, *The Elizabethan Underworld* (London: J. M. Dent, 1997); Catharine F. Seigel, "Hands Off The Hothouses: Shakespeare's Advice to the King," *Journal of Popular Culture* 20 (1986): 81-88;

J. A. Sharpe, *Crime in Early Modern England 1550-1750* (London: Longman, 1984); Kevin P. Siena, "Pollution, Promiscuity, and the Pox"; Wallace Shugg, "Prostitution in Shakespeare's London," *Shakespeare Studies* 10 (1977): 291-313; and Lawrence Stone, *The Family, Sex and Marriage in England 1500-1800* (New York: Harper & Row, 1977).

For more general histories of prostitution see Harry Benjamin and R. E. L. Masters, *Prostitution and Morality: A definitive report on the prostitute in contemporary society and an analysis of the causes and effects of the suppression of prostitution* (London: Souvenir, 1965); Vern L. Bullough, *The History of Prostitution* (New York: University Books, 1964); Burford, *Bawds and Lodgings* and *The Orrible Synne: A Look at London Lechery from Roman to Cromwellian Times* (London: Calder & Boyars, 1973); Hilary Evans, *Harlots, Whores & Hookers: A History of Prostitution* (New York: Taplinger, 1979); Fernando Henriques, *Prostitution and Society*, 2 vols. (London: MacGibbon & Kee, 1963); and George Ryley Scott, *Ladies of Vice: A History of Prostitution from Antiquity to the Present Day* (London: Tallis, 1968).

41. St. Augustine, *Divine Providence and the Problem of Evil (De ordine)*, in *Writings of Saint Augustine*, vol. 1 (New York: CIMA Publishing Company, 1948), II.iv.12; and St. Thomas Aquinas, *The Summa Theologica*, Great Books of the Western World No. 20, ed. Robert Maynard Hutchins et al., trans. Fathers of the English Dominican Province, revised by Daniel J. Sullivan (Chicago: Encyclopedia Britannica, 1952), Part 2, Q. 10, Art. 11, p. 436. Benjamin and Masters quote Aquinas as also stating, "'Prostitution in the towns is like the cesspool in the palace. Do away with the cesspool, and the palace will become and unclean and stinking place'" (*Prostitution and Morality*, 51). They give no note, and I have been unable to locate the source of their translation.

42. Karras, *Common Women*, 32.

43. Salisbury-Jones, *Street Life*, 149. Salgādo "Originally a stew was a sweating or steam-bath, a legacy from the Roman conquest. The association between such baths and bawdy houses was already common in Rome and was doubtless reinforced by the practice of sweating as a cure for venereal disease. Bankside was Stews' Bank by the time of Henry VIII and stews became a general term for brothels in Elizabethan England" (*Elizabethan Underworld*, 52).

44. Steven Mullaney, *The Place of the Stage: License, Play, and Power in Renaissance England* (Chicago: University of Chicago Press, 1988), 22.

45. Haselkorn, *Prostitution*, 9.

46. Benjamin and Masters, *Prostitution and Morality*, 59.

47. Bullough, *History of Prostitution*, 114.

48. Haselkorn, *Prostitution*, 9.

49. Chancellor, *Pleasure Haunts*, 170.

50. Archer, *Pursuit of Stability*, 252.

51. A. C. Hamilton, *The Structure of Allegory in "The Faerie Queene"* (Oxford: Clarendon Press, 1961), 49.

52. Carlin, *Medieval Southwark*, 40.

53. Haselkorn, *Prostitution*, 11; Johnson, *Southwark and the City*, 66; Margaret Pelling, "Appearances and Reality: Barber Surgeons, the Body and Disease," in *London 1500-1700: The Making of the Metropolis*, ed. A. L. Beier and Roger Findlay (London: Longman, 1986), 87; and Salisbury-Jones, *Street Life*, 149.

54. Griffiths, "Structure of Prostitution," 43; and Dean Stanton Barnard, Jr., ed., *Hollands Leaguer by Nicholas Goodman: A Critical Edition* (The Hague: Mouton, 1970; reprint of 1632 edition), 36-37. For Henry's proclamation, see *Tudor Royal Proclamations*, ed. Paul L. Hughes and James F. Larkin (New Haven: Yale University Press, 1964), 365-66.

55. Salgādo, *Elizabethan Underworld*, 52.

56. Shugg, "Prostitution in Shakespeare's London," 295.

57. Burford, *Bawds and Lodgings*, 147; and *The Orrible Synne*, 167.

58. Hugh Latimer, *Sermons by Hugh Latimer*, Parker Society No. 27, ed. George Elwes Corrie (Cambridge: Cambridge University Press, 1844), Third Sermon, 133-34.

59. Michel Foucault, *The History of Sexuality Volume I: An Introduction*, trans. Robert Hurley (New York: Pantheon, 1978), 44-45.

60. A. C. Hamilton, "A Theological Reading of *The Faerie Queene*, Book II," *ELH* 25 (1958): 161.

61. C. G. Jung, "Animus and Anima," in *Collected Works*, vol. 7, ed. Sir

Herbert Read et al., trans. R. F. C. Hull (London: Routledge & Kegan Paul, 1953), par. 338.

62. Gareth Roberts, "Circe," in *The Spenser Encyclopedia*, 165.

63. Margot Norris, "Disenchanting Enchantment: The Theatrical Brothel of 'Circe,'" in *Ulysses—En-Gendered Perspectives: Eighteen New Essays on the Episodes*, ed. Kimberly J. Devlin and Marilyn Reizbaum (Columbia: University of South Carolina Press, 1999), 229.

64. Maurice Evans, "Guyon and the Bower of Sloth," *Studies in Philology* 61 (1964): 144. As I point out in "Gertrude's Mermaid Allusion," mermaid is Elizabethan slang for prostitute (*British and American Studies* 2 [1999]: 20).

65. Shugg, "Prostitution in Shakespeare's London," 296.

66. Burford, *Bawds and Lodgings*, 142.

67. Salgãdo, *Elizabethan Underworld*, 54.

68. Rendle, "Stews on Bankside," 71.

69. Many of these quotations are assembled into Salgãdo's argument on 53-57. The passages can also be found as follows: "Lanthorn and Candelight," in Judges, *The Elizabethan Underworld*, 347; *The Honest Whore*, Part One, II.i.324-30, in *The Dramatic Works of Thomas Dekker*, ed. Fredson Bowers (Cambridge: University Press, 1955), 2:53; and Philip Stubbs, *The Anatomy of Abuses in Shakespeare's Youth* (New York: Johnson Reprint Corporation, 1972).

70. Robert Greene, "A Disputation Between a He-Cony-Catcher and a She-Cony-Catcher," in Judges, *The Elizabethan Underworld*, 206.

71. Roberts, "Circe," 166.

72. Kelly, "Bishops, Prioress, and Bawd," 379; and Johnson, *Southwark and the City*, 67.

73. Stow, *Survey of London*, 371.

74. Graziani, "*The Faerie Queene*, Book II," 276.

75. Anderson, "Prostitution's Artful Guise," 110.

76. Carlin, *Medieval Southwark*, 347.

77. Sheila T. Cavanagh, "Nightmares of Desire: Evil Women in *The Faerie Queene*," *Studies in Philology* 91 (1994): 322.

78. Thomas Nashe, *Christs Teares Over Jerusalem* (1593), in *Works of Thomas Nashe*, ed. Ronald B. McKerrow (Oxford: Basil Blackwell, 1966), 2:153.

79. W. W. Greg, "The Damnation of Faustus," *Modern Language Notes* 41 (1946): 106.

80. Frye, *Educated Imagination*, 64.

81. Shugg, "Prostitution in Shakespeare's London," 301.

82. N. S. Brook, "C. S. Lewis and Spenser: Nature, Art and the Bower of Bliss" (1949), in *Essential Articles for the Study of Edmund Spenser*, ed. A. C. Hamilton (Hamden, Conn.: Archon, 1972), 23-24.

83. Castiglione makes a similar statement: "And thus it [physical beauty] attracts itself to the gaze of others, and entering through their eyes it impresses itself upon the human soul, which it stirs and lights with its charm, inflaming it with passion and desire. Thus the mind is seized by desire for the beauty which it recognizes as good, and, if it allows itself to be guided by what its senses tell it, it falls into the gravest errors and judges that the body is the chief cause of the beauty which it enshrines, and so to enjoy that beauty it must necessarily achieve with it as intimate a union as possible" (*The Book of the Courtier*, trans. George Bull [New York: Penguin, 1967], 326).

84. Berger, *Allegorical Temper*, 218.

85. Shugg, "Prostitution in Shakespeare's London," 295.

86. McMullan, *Canting Crew*, 135.

87. Miller, "Phaedria," 34.

88. Barnard, "Introduction," in *Hollands Leaguer*, 42; Hyder E. Rollins, ed., *A Pepsyian Garland: Black-Letter Broadside Ballads of the Years 1595-1639 Chiefly from the Collection of Samuel Pepys* (Cambridge: University Press, 1922), 399.

89. Shugg, "Prostitution in Shakespeare's London," 297.

90. Barnard, in *Hollands Leaguer*, 7-9, 44, 46, 123.

91. Haselkorn, *Prostitution*, 11-12; Judges, *Elizabethan Underworld*, 513, n. 26; Lindley, 110; and Rendle, "Stews on Bankside," 76-77.

92. Judges, ibid; and Harris, "Bawdy House Riots," 554.

93. Beier and Finlay, "Introduction: The Significance of the Metropolis," in *Making of the Metropolis*, 22.

94. Harris, "Bawdy House Riots," 543.

95. Freud, "Totem and Taboo," in *Standard Edition*, 13:35. Stephen Greenblatt echoes Freud: "Guyon's destructive act" is "a painful sexual renunciation . . . we are invited to experience the ontogeny of our culture's violent resistance to a sensuous release for which it nevertheless yearns with a new intensity." Here Greenblatt recapitulates Freud's ideas of "renunciation" and ambivalent emotions ("violent resistance" vs. "yearns"). His later statement that the razing of the bower is "seemingly intemperate" evidently implies that its essence is continence (reason over desire). See *Renaissance Self-Fashioning: From More to Shakespeare* (Chicago: University of Chicago Press, 1980), 175, 177.

96. Stone, *Family, Sex and Marriage*, 619.

97. Berger, *Allegorical Temper*, 218; and Harriett Hankins, *Poetic Freedom and Poetic Truth: Chaucer, Shakespeare, Marlowe, Milton* (Oxford: Clarendon Press, 1976), 73.

98. Prostitutes were pilloried, carted, whipped, dunked, imprisoned, publicly disgraced (forced to carry a white rod or wear a striped hood), banished, and had their heads shaved (see Karras, *Common Women*, 15; and Burford, *The Orryble Sinne*, 97-98). For *accabussade* (dunking a naked prostitute three times in a cage so that she nearly drowns) see Evans, *Harlots*, 56-57. The analogy between Acrasia's being sent to the Faerie Queene's court in Book III, Canto 1, and the carting of prostitutes is weak; the former is really a nonpunishment because Spenser never describes it being carried out.

99. Miller, "Phaedria," 44.

100. Hamilton, *The Structure of Allegory*, 132.

101. Madelon S. Gohlke, "Embattled Allegory: Book II of *The Faerie Queene*," *English Literary Renaissance* 8 (1978): 137.

102. Hamilton, "'Like Race To Runne,'" 334; and Laura Mulvey, *Visual and Other Pleasures* (London: Macmillan, 1989), 8.

Chapter Five

1. William Blackburn, "Spenser's Merlin," *Renaissance and Reformation* N.S. 4 (1980): 186, 191.

2. Patrick Gerard Cheney, "'Secret Power Unseene': Good Magic in Spenser's Legend of Britomart," *Studies in Philology* 85 (1988): 8.

3. As Thomas P. Roche, Jr., points out in his note on the stanza, it is not Hercules but Theseus who slays the Centaurs (*The Faerie Queene* [New Haven: Yale University Press, 1981], 1167). Roche cites Ovid, *Metamorphoses* 12.210ff. and *The Faerie Queene* VI.x.13. Cf. Boccaccio, *Genealogy of the Gods* 9.28.

4. In Hesiod's *Theogony*, she is the granddaughter of Night, which would make her Duessa's cousin. In fact, it is Duessa who in Book IV "raised [her] from below, / Out of the dwellings of the damned sprights, / Where she in darknes wastes her cursed daies & nights" (IV.i.19). As a descendant of Night, Ate is related not only to Aveugle (darkness or blindness) but also to the ignorance and malignity that C. W. Lemmi calls "the night of the mind," from which all human ills descend (*Variorum*, 1:231).

5. Blackburn, "Spenser's Merlin," 182.

6. Andrew Fichter, *Poets Historical: Dynastic Epic in the Renaissance* (New Haven: Yale University Press, 1982), 172-73. Fichter cites Joshua 10:12, 2 Kings 20:10, Judges 7, and Matthew 21:21.

7. Thomas E. Maresca, *Three English Epics* (Lincoln: University of Nebraska Press, 1979), 51.

8. Cf. the genealogy in the *Variorum*, 1:230.

9. Discord presents primarily a verbal threat to friendship, as the portrayal of Nimrod on the tapestry in Ate's cave attests. As the main builder of the tower of Babel, Nimrod fuels discord by actions leading to the disruption of language. In a similar way, discord in the middle books of *The Faerie Queene* manifests itself in such words as Paridell and Blandamour exchange over the false Florimell,

the secret lovers' language that Paridell and Hellenore speak, and Ate's own indictment of Duessa at Mercilla's court. Discord feeds on words, which is why Ate is described as a verbal cannibal:

> For life it is to her, when others sterue
> Through mischieuous debate, and deadly feood,
> That she may sucke their life, and drinke their blood,
> With which she from her childhood had bene fed. (IV.i.26)

Her assault calls to mind other verbal attempts to disrupt human relations: Duessa's letter in Book I and scandal in Book VI. Appropriately, Ate and Duessa accompany Paridell and Blandamour, and Ate's "euill wordes" (25) stem from "Her lying tongue [that] was in two parts diuided, / And both the parts did speake, and both contended" (27). The detail anticipates the Blatant Beast whose false tongues number either a hundred or a thousand (V.xii.41; VI.i.9, xii.27).

10. A. Bartlett Giamatti, *Play of Double Senses: Spenser's* Faerie Queene (Englewood Cliffs, N.J.: Prentice Hall, 1975), 120.

11. J. A. MacCulloch, *The Harrowing of Hell: A Comparative Study of an Early Christian Doctrine* (Edinburgh: T. & T. Clark, 1930), 219.

12. Thomas P. Roche, Jr., *The Kindly Flame: A Study of the Third and Fourth Books of Spenser's* Faerie Queene (Princeton: Princeton University Press, 1964), 53-54. For parallel passages see Merritt Y. Hughes, *Virgil and Spenser*, (Berkeley: University of California Press, 1929), 348-53.

13. For a related point, see James Nohrnberg, *The Analogy of* The Faerie Queene (Princeton: Princeton University Press, 1976), 433.

14. Cheney, "Secret Power," 16.

15. C. S Lewis, *Spenser's Images of Life*, ed. Alastair Fowler (Cambridge: Cambridge University Press, 1965), 66.

16. Merlin's chronicle of British kings, which begins with Artegall and ends with Elizabeth, completes the history of England found in Book III, Canto 9 (the fall of Troy to the founding of Troynovant), and Book II, Canto 10 (Brutus to Uther Pendragon). As Fichter points out, Merlin's prophecy tells the story of the "exile of the Britons and the eventual restoration of their line in the person of Henry VII, the first of the Tudor monarchs" (*Poets Historical*, 175). Fichter acknowledges, however, that "the last event in British history mentioned by Merlin seems strangely out of line with the prophecy of an era of 'sacred Peace' under Henry VII"—the "white rod" of war wielded against "the great Castle" (Castile), a reference to the English defeat of the Spanish Armada (179). In a

similar way, Harry Berger, Jr., divides Merlin's prophecy into three sections that move toward the moral ambiguity of the English people in a later age: Merlin first describes a period of history in which might prevails and moral issues are well defined (stanzas 26-34); in the second section, moral issues are less clear-cut, deception plays a role in conflicts, and the reasons for war are ambiguous because the enemy is Christian (stanzas 35-42); and finally, in stanzas 43-50, the Britons' supremacy has passed, and they are assimilated into a political structure uniting warring nations under Elizabeth ("The Structure of Merlin's Chronicle in *The Faerie Queene* III [iii]," *Studies in English Literature 1500-1900* 9 [1969]: 39-51). For more recent treatments, see Howard Dobin, *Merlin's Disciples: Prophecy, Poetry, and Power in Renaissance England* (Stanford, Calif.: Stanford University Press, 1990), and Susanne Lindgren Wofford, *The Choice of Achilles: The Ideology of Figure in the Epic* (Stanford, Calif.: Stanford University Press, 1992), 274-81.

17. Nohrnberg points out that in *The Ruines of Time*, lines 372-78, Spenser attributes to the Muses (and thus to the poet) the power to harrow hell (*Analogy*, 677).

18. Blackburn, "Spenser's Merlin," 182.

Chapter Six

1. Thomas E. Maresca, *Three English Epics* (Lincoln: University of Nebraska Press, 1979), 14, 34.

2. Thomas E. Maresca, "Hell," in *The Spenser Encyclopedia*, ed. A. C. Hamilton et al. (Toronto: University of Toronto Press, 1990), 352.

3. For these three terms, see Joseph Campbell, *The Hero with a Thousand Faces*, Bollingen Ser. 17, 2d ed. (Princeton: Princeton University Press, 1973). A helpful discussion of the hero's journey appears in Charles A. Huttar, "Hell and The City: Tolkien and the Traditions of Western Literature," in *A Tolkien Compass*, ed. Jared Lobdell (La Salle, Ill.: Open Court, 1975), 117-42.

4. Maresca, *Three English Epics*, 24, 26.

5. Ibid., 44.

6. Robert Ellrodt, *Neoplatonism in the Poetry of Spenser* (Geneva: Librairie E. Droz, 1960), 77; Josephine Waters Bennett, "Spenser's Garden of Adonis," *PMLA* 47 (1932): 51; and James Nohrnberg, *The Analogy of* The Faerie Queene (Princeton: Princeton University Press, 1976), 554-55.

7. In "Ruines of Rome," line 308, Spenser also mentions "great *Chaos* wombe." Cf. *FQ* IV.ii.47:

> Farre vnder ground from tract of liuing went,
> Downe in the bottome of the deepe *Abysse*,
> Where *Demogorgon* in dull darknesse pent,
> Farre from the view of Gods and heauens blis,
> The hideous *Chaos* keepes, their [the Fates'] dreadfull dwelling is.

8. Elizabeth Bieman, *Plato Baptized: Towards the Interpretation of Spenser's Mimetic Fictions* (Toronto: Univeristy of Toronto Press, 1988), 221.

9. Bennett, "Spenser's Garden," 50.

10. Virgil, *Aeneid*, trans. Allen Mandelbaum (New York: Bantam, 1978). This material is quoted with the permission of Bantam Books, a division of Random House, Inc.

11. Thomas J. J. Altizer, *The Descent into Hell: A Study of the Radical Reversal of the Christian Consciousness* (Philadelphia: J. B. Lippincott, 1970), 116-17.

12. Nohrnberg, *Analogy*, 442-44.

13. Huttar, "Hell and The City," 123.

14. Homer, *Odyssey*, trans. Richmond Lattimore (New York: Harper & Row, 1965), 11:134-36. This material is quoted with the permission of HarperCollins Publishers.

15. Nohrnberg notes that Scudamore is to Amoret as Orpheus is to Eurydice in III.xii.19 and IV.x.58 (*Analogy*, 489).

16. John M. Steadman, "Milton and Patristic Tradition: The Quality of Hell Fire," *Anglia* 76 (1958): 116.

17. Harold L. Weatherby, *Mirrors of Celestial Grace: Patristic Theology in Spenser's Allegory* (Toronto: University of Toronto Press, 1994), 192.

18. The same sense is present in Book IV: her face, like Arthur's shield, "plainely did expresse / The heauenly pourtraict of bright Angels hew" (v.13).

BIBLIOGRAPHY

Primary Sources

Alighieri, Dante. *The Divine Comedy*, trans. C. H. Sisson. Chicago: Gateway, 1980.

Aquinas, Thomas. *The Summa Theologica*. Great Books of the Western World No. 20, ed. Robert Maynard Hutchins et al., trans. Fathers of the English Dominican Province. Revised by Daniel J. Sullivan. Chicago: Encyclopedia Britannica, 1981.

Atkinson, David William. "The English Ars Morendi [*sic*]: Its Protestant Transformation." *Renaissance and Reformation* N.S. 6 (1982): 1-10.

Atkinson, David William, ed. *The English* Ars Moriendi. New York: Peter Lang, 1992.

Augustine. *Confessions*, trans. J. G. Pilkington. In *Nicene and Post-Nicene Fathers*, ed. Philip Schaff, vol. 1. Peabody, Mass.: Hendrickson Publishers, 1995.

---. *Divine Providence and the Problem of Evil (De ordine)*. In *Writings of Saint Augustine*, vol. 1. New York: CIMA Publishing Company, 1948.

Barnard, Dean Stanton, Jr., ed. *Hollands Leaguer by Nicholas Goodman: A Critical Edition* (1632). The Hague: Mouton, 1970.

Becon, Thomas. *The Catechism of Thomas Becon, With Other Pieces Written by Him in the Reign of King Edward the Sixth*. Parker Society No. 3, ed. John Ayre. Cambridge: Cambridge University Press, 1844.

---. *The Sicke Mans Salve* (1561). In Atkinson, *The English* Ars Moriendi, 87-126.

---. "The Sick Man's Salve." *Prayers and Other Pieces of Thomas Becon*. Folio edition 1561. Parker Society No. 4, ed. John Ayre. Cambridge: Cambridge University Press, 1844.

Bilson, Thomas. *The effect of certaine Sermons Tovching the Fvll Redemption of mankind by the death and bloud of Christ Jesus*. London: Peter Short, 1599.

Burton, Robert. *The Anatomy of Melancholy*, ed. Floyd Dell and Paul Jordan-Smith. New York: Tudor, 1938.

Calvin, John. *The Institutes of the Christian* Religion, ed. John T. McNeill, trans. Ford Lewis Battles, vol. 1. The Library of Christian Classics. Philadelphia: Westminster, 1960.

Castiglione, Baldesar. *The Book of the Courtier*, trans. George Bull. New York: Penguin, 1967.

Caxton, William, trans. *The Arte & Crafte to Know Well to Dye* (1490). In Atkinson, *The English* Ars Moriendi, 21-36.

Comes, Natalis. *Mythologiae*. New York: Garland Publishing, 1976.

Coryate, Thomas. *Coryat's Crudities* (1611). Glasgow: Robert Maclehose, 1905.

Cranmer, Thomas. "Corrections of the Institution of a Christian Man, by Henry VIII. With Archbishop Cranmer's Annotations" (1538). In *Miscellaneous Writings and Letters of Thomas Cranmer*. Parker Society No. 16, ed. John Edmund Cox. Cambridge: Cambridge University Press, 1846.

Dekker, Thomas. *The Honest Whore*, Part One. In *The Dramatic Works of Thomas Dekker*, ed. Fredson Bowers, vol. 2. Cambridge: Cambridge University Press, 1955.

Erasmus, Desiderius. *Preparatione to Deathe* (1534). In Atkinson, *The English* Ars Moriendi, 37-68.

Freud, Sigmund. *The Standard Edition of the Complete Psychological Works*, ed. and trans. James Strachey. London: Hogarth Press, 1966.

Geneva Bible: A Facsimile of the 1560 Edition. Madison: University of Wisconsin Press, 1969.

"Grace." *The Oxford Dictionary of the Christian Church*, ed. F. L. Cross and E. A. Livingstone. London: Oxford University Press, 1974.

Greene, Robert. "A Disputation Between a He-Cony-Catcher and a She-Cony

Catcher" (1592). In Judges, *The Elizabethan Underworld*, 206-47.

"The Harrowing of Hell." *The Exeter Book.* Part 2. Early English Text Society No. 194, ed. W. S. Mackie. London: Oxford University Press, 1934.

Here Begynneth the Treatys of Nicodemus Gospel. N.p., 1532.

Hesiod. *Theogony*, trans. Norman O. Brown. New York: Liberal Arts Press, 1953.

Hill, Adam. *The Defence of the Article: Christ Descended into Hell.* London, 1592.

Homer, *Odyssey*, trans. Richmond Lattimore. New York: Harper & Row, 1965.

Hughes, Paul L., and James F. Larkin, eds. *Tudor Royal Proclamations.* New Haven: Yale University Press, 1964.

Judges, A. V., ed. *The Elizabethan Underworld.* London: George Routledge, 1930.

Jung, C. G. *The Collected Works*, ed. Sir Herbert Read et al., trans. R. F. C. Hull. London: Routledge & Kegan Paul, 1953.

Langland, William. *Piers the Ploughman*, ed. J. F. Goodridge. Baltimore: Penguin, 1959.

Latimer, Hugh. *Sermons.* Parker Society No. 27, ed. George Elwes Corrie. Cambridge: Cambridge University Press, 1844.

Longland, John. *A Sermond [sic] spoken before the kynge his maiestie at Grenwiche, vppon good fryday: the yere of our Lord 1536.* London: T. Petyt, 1538.

Lupset, Thomas. *The Waye of Dyenge Well* (1538). In Atkinson, *The English* Ars Moriendi, 69-86.

Maclean, Hugh, ed. *A Norton Critical Edition: Edmund Spenser's Poetry.* New York: Norton, 1968.

The Middle-English Harrowing of Hell and Gospel of Nicodemus, ed. William Henry Hulme. London: Oxford University Press, 1961.

Milton, John. *Areopagitica*. In *Complete Prose Works of John Milton*, ed. Ernest Sirluck et al., vol. 2. New Haven: Yale University Press, 1959.

Nashe, Thomas. *Christs Teares Over Jerusalem* (1593). In *Works of Thomas Nashe*, ed. Ronald B. McKerrow, vol. 2. Oxford: Basil Blackwell, 1966.

Ovid. *Metamorphoses*, trans. Mary M. Innes. New York: Penguin, 1955.

Ovide Moralisé, ed. C. De Boer et al., vol. 3. Amsterdam: Uitgave van de N. V. Noord-Hollandsche Uitgeversmaatschappij, 1931.

Pearson, John. *An Exposition of the Creed* (1659). 8th ed. London: n.p., 1704.

Perkins, William. *A Salve for a Sicke Man* (1595). In Atkinson, *The English* Ars Moriendi, 127-64.

Plutarch. *The Lives*, trans. Sir Thomas North, vol. 1. Reprint of 1579 ed. New York: AMS Press, 1967.

Rollins, Hyder E., ed. *A Pepsyian Garland: Black-Letter Broadside Ballads of the Years 1595-1639 Chiefly from the Collection of Samuel Pepys*. Cambridge: University Press, 1922.

Rouse, W. H. D. *Shakespeare's Ovid: Being Arthur Golding's Translation of the "Metamorphoses"*. Carbondale: Southern Illinois University Press, 1961.

Rylands, W. Harry, ed. *The Ars Moriendi (ca. 1450), A Reproduction of the Copy in the British Museum*. London: Wyman & Sons, 1881.

Shakespeare, William. *Hamlet*. In *The Complete Works of Shakespeare*, ed. David Bevington, 4th ed. New York: HarperCollins, 1992.

Spenser, Edmund. *The Complete Poetical Works of Edmund Spenser: Cambridge Edition*, ed. R. E. Neil Dodge. Boston: Houghton Mifflin, 1908.

---. *The Poetical Works of Edmund Spenser*, ed. J. C. Smith and E. de Selincourt. London: Oxford, 1932.

---. *The Faerie Queene*, Book I, ed. P. C. Bayley. Oxford: Oxford University Press, 1966.

---. *The Faerie Queene*, ed. A. C. Hamilton. New York: Longman, 1977.

---. *The Faerie Queene*, ed. Thomas P. Roche, Jr., with C. Patrick O'Donnell, Jr. New Haven: Yale University Press, 1981.

---. *Spenser's* Faerie Queene*: A New Edition, with a Glossary, and Notes Explanatory and Critical*, ed. John Upton. London: J. and R. Tonson, 1758.

---. *The Works of Edmund Spenser: A Variorum Edition*, ed. Edwin Greenlaw et al. 10 vols. Baltimore: Johns Hopkins University Press, 1932-36.

Statius, *Thebiad*, trans. A. D. Melville. Oxford: Clarendon Press, 1992.

Stow, John. *A Survey of London* (1558), ed. Henry Morley. Dover, N.H.: Sutton, 1994.

Stubbs, Philip. *The Anatomy of Abuses in Shakespeare's Youth* (1583). New York: Johnson Reprint Corporation, 1972.

The Thirty-Nine Articles of Religion. Available at the following website: http://web.singnet.com.sg/~kohfly/articles.html.

Virgil. *Aeneid*, trans. Allen Mandelbaum. New York: Bantam, 1971.

Secondary Sources on Spenser

Alpers, Paul. *The Poetry of the Faerie Queene*. Princeton: Princeton University Press, 1967.

Anderson, Judith. *The Growth of a Personal Voice: "Piers Plowman" and "The Faerie Queene"*. New Haven: Yale University Press, 1976.

---. "Redcrosse and the Descent into Hell." *ELH* 36 (1969): 470-92.

Bennett, Josephine Waters. "Spenser's Garden of Adonis." *PMLA* 47 (1932): 46-80.

Berger, Harry, Jr. *The Allegorical Temper: Vision and Reality in Book II of Spenser's Faerie Queene*. New Haven: Yale University Press, 1957.

---. "The Structure of Merlin's Chronicle in *The Faerie Queene* III [iii]." *Studies in English Literature 1500-1900* 9 (1969): 39-51.

144

Bieman, Elizabeth. *Plato Baptized: Towards the Interpretation of Spenser's Mimetic Fictions*. Toronto: University of Toronto Press, 1988.

Blackburn, William. "Spenser's Merlin." *Renaissance and Reformation* N.S. 4 (1980): 179-98.

Blissett, William. "Caves, Labyrinths, and *The Faerie Queene*." *Unfolded Tales: Essays on Renaissance Romance*, ed. George Logan and Gordon Teskey. Ithaca: Cornell University Press, 1989.

Brooke, N. S. "C. S. Lewis and Spenser: Nature, Art and the Bower of Bliss." In Hamilton, *Essential Articles*, 13-28.

Bulger, Thomas F. "Classical Vision and Christian Revelation: Spenser's Use of Mythology in Book I of *The Faerie Queene*." *Greyfriar* 23 (1982): 5-25.

Cavanagh, Sheila T. "Nightmares of Desire: Evil Women in *The Faerie Queene*." *Studies in Philology* 91 (1994): 313-38.

Cheney, Donald. *Spenser's Image of Nature: Wild Man and Shepherd in "The Faerie Queene"*. New Haven: Yale University Press, 1966.

Cheney, Patrick Gerard. "'Secret Powre Unseene': Good Magic in Spenser's Legend of Britomart." *Studies in Philology* 85 (1988): 1-28.

Cullen, Patrick. *The Infernal Triad: The Flesh, the World, and the Devil in Spenser and Milton*. Princeton: Princeton University Press, 1974.

Ellrodt, Robert. *Neoplatonism in the Poetry of Spenser*. Geneva: Librairie E. Droz, 1960.

Evans, Maurice. "The Fall of Guyon." *ELH* 28 (1961): 215-24.

---. "Guyon and the Bower of Sloth." *Studies in Philology* 61 (1964): 140-49.

Fichter, Andrew. *Poets Historical: Dynastic Epic in the Renaissance*. New Haven: Yale University Press, 1982.

Fletcher, Angus. *The Prophetic Moment: An Essay on Spenser*. Chicago: University of Chicago Press, 1971.

Giamatti, A. Bartlett. *Play of Double Senses: Spenser's* Faerie Queene. Englewood Cliffs, N.J.: Prentice Hall, 1975.

Gless, Darryl J. *Interpretation and Theology in Spenser*. Cambridge: Cambridge University Press, 1994.

Gohlke, Madelon S. "Embattled Allegory: Book II of *The Faerie Queene*." *English Literary Renaissance* 8 (1978): 123-40.

Graziani, René. "*The Faerie Queene*, Book II." In Hamilton, *The Spenser Encyclopedia*, 263-70.

Greenblatt, Stephen. *Renaissance Self-Fashioning: From More to Shakespeare*. Chicago: University of Chicago Press, 1980.

Hamilton, A. C. "'Like Race To Runne': The Parallel Structure of *The Faerie Queene*, Books I and II." *PMLA* 73 (1958): 327-34.

---. "On Annotating Spenser's *Faerie Queene*: A New Approach to The Poem." In *Contemporary Thought on Edmund Spenser*, ed. Richard C. Frushell and Bernard J. Vondersmith. Carbondale: Southern Illinois University Press, 1975.

---. "Spenser's Treatment of Myth." *ELH* 26 (1959): 335-54.

---. *The Structure of Allegory in "The Faerie Queene"*. Oxford: Clarendon Press, 1961.

---. "A Theological Reading of *The Faerie Queene*, Book II." *ELH* 25 (1958): 155-62.

Hamilton, A. C., ed. *Essential Articles for the Study of Edmund Spenser*. Hamden, Conn.: Archon, 1972.

Hamilton, A. C., et al., eds. *The Spenser Encyclopedia*. Toronto: University of Toronto Press, 1990.

Hankins, Harriett. *Poetic Freedom and Poetic Truth: Chaucer, Shakespeare, Marlowe, Milton*. Oxford: Clarendon Press, 1976.

Hankins, John E. "Psychomachia." In Hamilton, *The Spenser Encyclopedia*, 570.

Hankins, John Erskine. *Source and Meaning in Spenser's Allegory: A Study of 'The Faerie Queene'*. Oxford: Oxford University Press, 1971.

Harris, Tim. "The Bawdy House Riots of 1668." *The Historical Journal* 29 (1986): 537-56.

Horton, Ronald A. "Dwarfs." In Hamilton, *The Spenser Encyclopedia*, 230.

---. "Virtues." In Hamilton, *The Spenser Encyclopedia*, 719-21.

Hosington, Brenda M. "Idle Lake." In Hamilton, *The Spenser Encyclopedia*, 387.

Hughes, Merritt Y. *Virgil and Spenser*. Berkeley: University of California Press, 1929.

Hume, Anthea. *Edmund Spenser: Protestant Poet*. Cambridge: Cambridge University Press, 1984.

Hunt, John Dixon, and Michael Leslie. "Gardens." In Hamilton, *The Spenser Encyclopedia*, 323-25.

Kaske, Carol, *Spenser and Biblical Poetics*. Ithaca: Cornell University Press, 1999.

Kermode, Frank. "The Cave of Mammon." *Stratford-on-Avon Studies* 2 (1960): 151-74. Reprinted in *Shakespeare, Spenser, Donne*. London: Routledge and Kegan Paul, 1971.

King, John N. *Spenser's Poetry and the Reformation Tradition*. Princeton: Princeton University Press, 1990.

Koller, Kathrine. "Art, Rhetoric, and Holy Dying in the *Faerie Queene* with Special Reference to the Despair Canto." *Studies in Philology* 61 (1964): 128-39.

Krier, Theresa M. *Gazing on Secret Sights: Spenser, Classical Imitation, and the Decorums of Vision*. Ithaca: Cornell University Press, 1990.

Lemmi, C. W. "The Symbolism of the Classical Episodes in *The Faerie Queene*." *Philological Quarterly* 8 (1929): 270-87.

Lewis, C. S. *Spenser's Images of Life*, ed. Alastair Fowler. Cambridge: Cambridge University Press, 1965.

Lockerd, Benjamin G., Jr. *The Sacred Marriage: Psychic Integration in "The Faerie Queene"*. London: Associated University Presses, 1987.

Lotspeich, Henry Gibbons. *Classical Mythology in the Poetry of Edmund Spenser*.

Princeton: Princeton University Press, 1932.

Maresca, Thomas E. "Hell." In Hamilton, *The Spenser Encyclopedia*, 351-52.

---. *Three English Epics*. Lincoln: University of Nebraska Press, 1979.

McKim, William M., Jr. "The Divine and Infernal Comedy of Spenser's Mammon," *Essays in Literature* 1 (1974): 3-16.

Miller, Lewis H., Jr. "Phaedria, Mammon, and Sir Guyon's Education by Error." *Journal of English and Germanic Philology* 63 (1964): 33-44.

Mounts, Charles E. "Spenser's Seven Bead-men and the Corporal Works of Mercy." *PMLA* 54 (1939): 974-80.

Neill, Kerby. "The Degradation of the Redcrosse Knight." *ELH* 19 (1952): 173-90.

Nellist, B. "The Allegory of Guyon's Voyage: An Interpretation." In Hamilton, *Essential Articles*, 238-52.

Nohrnberg, James. *The Analogy of* The Faerie Queene. Princeton: Princeton University Press, 1976.

Osgood, Charles Grosvenor. *A Concordance to the Poems of Edmund Spenser*. Carnegie Institution of Washington Publications, Philadelphia: J. B. Lippincott, 1915.

Pearson, D'Orsay W. "Spenser's Labyrinth--Again." *Studies in Iconography* 3 (1977): 70-88.

---. "Theseus, Hippolytus." In Hamilton, *The Spenser Encyclopedia*, 686.

Reid, Robert L. "Holiness, house of." In Hamilton, *The Spenser Encyclopedia*, 373-74.

Roberts, Gareth. "Circe." In Hamilton, *The Spenser Encyclopedia,* 165-67.

Roche, Thomas P., Jr. *The Kindly Flame: A Study of the Third and Fourth Books of Spenser's* Faerie Queene. Princeton: Princeton University Press, 1964.

Schiavoni, James. "Predestination and Free Will: The Crux of Canto 10." *Spenser Studies* 10 (1992): 175-95.

Schoenfeldt, Michael. *Bodies and Selves in Early Modern England: Physiology and Inwardness in Spenser, Shakespeare, Herbert, and Milton.* Cambridge: Cambridge University Press, 1999.

Sessions, William A. "Spenser's Georgics." *English Literary Renaissance* 10 (1980): 202-38.

Skulsky, Harold. "Spenser's Despair Episode and the Theology of Doubt." *Modern Philology* 78 (1981): 227-42.

Shaheen, Naseeb. *Biblical References in* The Faerie Queene. Memphis: Memphis State University Press, 1976.

Sirluck, Ernest. "The *Faerie Queene,* Book II, and the *Nicomachean Ethics.*" *Modern Philology* 49 (1951): 73-100.

---. "A Note on the Rhetoric of Spenser's Despair." *Modern Philology* 47 (1949): 8-11.

Teskey, Gordon. "Arthur in *The Faerie Queene.*" In Hamilton, *The Spenser Encyclopedia,* 69-71.

Waters, Douglas. *Duessa As Theological Satire.* Columbia, Mo.: University of Missouri Press, 1970.

Waters, Josephine Bennett. "Spenser's Garden of Adonis." *PMLA* 47 (1932): 46-80.

Weatherby, Harold L. "*Axiochus.*" In Hamilton, *The Spenser Encyclopedia,* 77.

---. *Mirrors of Celestial Grace: Patristic Theology in Spenser's Allegory.* Toronto: University of Toronto Press, 1994.

Webb, W. S. "Vergil in Spenser's Epic Theory." In *Critical Essays on Spenser from ELH,* 1-23. Baltimore: n.p., 1970.

Whitaker, Virgil K. *The Religious Basis of Spenser's Thought* (1950). New York: Gordian, 1966.

Wofford, Susanne Lindgren. *The Choice of Achilles: The Ideology of Figure in the Epic.* Stanford, Calif.: Stanford University Press, 1992.

Woodhouse, A. S. P. "Nature and Grace in *The Faerie Queene.*" In Hamilton,

Essential Articles, 58-83.

Other Secondary Sources

Altizer, Thomas J. J. *The Descent Into Hell: A Study of the Radical Reversal of the Christian Consciousness*. Philadelphia: J. B. Lippincott, 1970.

Anderson, Amanda. "Prostitution's Artful Guise." Review of Charles *Bernheimer's Figures of Ill Repute: Representing Prostitution in Nineteenth-Century France*. In *Diacritics: A Review of Contemporary Criticism* 21 (1991): 102-22.

Andre, Caroline S. "Some Selected Aspects of the Role of Women in Sixteenth Century England." *International Journal of Women's Studies* 4 (1981): 76-88.

Archer, Ian W. *The Pursuit of Stability: Social Relations in Elizabethan London*. Cambridge: Cambridge University Press, 1991.

Babb, Lawrence. *The Elizabethan Malady: A Study of Melancholia in English Literature from 1580 to 1642*. East Lansing: Michigan State College Press, 1951.

Beaty, Nancy Lee. *The Craft of Dying: A Study in the Literary Tradition of the* Ars Moriendi *in England*. Yale Studies in English No. 175. New Haven: Yale University Press, 1970.

Benjamin, Harry, and R. E. L. Masters. *Prostitution and Morality: A definitive report on the prostitute in contemporary society and an analysis of the cause and effects of the suppression of prostitution*. London: Souvenir, 1965.

Berlin, Normand. *The Base String: The Underworld in Elizabethan Drama*. Rutherford: Fairleigh Dickinson University Press, 1968.

Bicknell, E. J. *A Theological Introduction to the Thirty-Nine Articles of the Church of England*. 3d ed. Revised by H. J. Carpenter. London: Longmans, 1963.

Bord, Janet. *Mazes and Labyrinths of the World*. New York: E. P. Dutton, 1975.

Bullough, Vern L. *The History of Prostitution*. New York: University Books, 1964.

Burford, E. J. *Bawds and Lodgings: A History of the London Bankside Brothels c. 100-1675.* London: Peter Owen, 1976.

---. *The Orrible Synne: A Look at London Lechery from Roman to Cromwellian Times.* London: Calder & Boyars, 1973.

Burke, E. M. "Grace." In *The New Catholic Encyclopedia.* New York: McGraw Hill, 1967.

Bush, Douglas. *Mythology and the Renaissance Tradition in English Poetry.* Minneapolis: University of Minnesota Press, 1932.

---. *Pagan Myth and Christian Tradition in English Poetry.* Philadelphia: American Philosophical Society, 1968.

Campbell, Jackson J. "To Hell and Back: Latin Tradition and Literary Use of the 'Descensus ad Inferos' in Old English." *Viator: Medieval and Renaissance Studies* 13 (1982): 107-58.

Campbell, Joseph. *The Hero with a Thousand Faces.* Bollingen Ser. 17, 2d ed. Princeton: Princeton University Press, 1973.

Carlin, Martha. *Medieval Southwark.* London: Hambledon, 1996.

Castledon, Rodney. *The Knossos Labyrinth: A New View of the "Palace of Minos" at Knossos.* London: Routledge, 1990.

Chancellor, E. Beresford. *The Pleasure Haunts of London During Four Centuries.* Boston: Houghton Mifflin, 1925.

Cressy, David. *Birth, Marriage, and Death: Ritual, Religion, and the Life-Cycle in Tudor and Stuart England.* New York: Oxford University Press, 1997.

Dobin, Howard. *Merlin's Disciples: Prophecy, Poetry, and Power in Renaissance England.* Stanford, Calif.: Stanford University Press, 1990.

Doebler, Bettie Anne. *Rooted Sorrow: Dying in Early Modern England.* Rutherford, N.J.: Fairleigh Dickinson University Press, 1994.

Doob, Penelope Reed. *The Idea of the Labyrinth from Classical Antiquity through the Middle Ages.* Ithaca: Cornell University Press, 1990.

Edwards, Ruth B. "The Story of Theseus." In *The Quest for Theseus*, ed. Anne G. Ward et al. New York: Praeger Publishers, 1970.

Evans, Hilary. *Harlots, Whores & Hookers: A History of Prostitution*. New York: Taplinger, 1979.

Feder, Lillian. *Ancient Myth in Modern Poetry*. Princeton: Princeton University Press, 1971.

Fike, Matthew A. "Gertrude's Mermaid Allusion." *British and American Studies* 2 (1999): 15-25.

Fletcher, Angus. "The Image of Lost Direction." *Centre and Labyrinth: Essays in Honour of Northrop Frye*, ed. Eleanor Cook et al. Toronto: University of Toronto Press, 1983.

Foucault, Michel. *The History of Sexuality Volume I: An Introduction*, trans. Robert Hurley. New York: Pantheon, 1978.

Frye, Northrop. *The Educated Imagination*. Bloomington: Indiana University Press, 1964.

Goodridge, J. F. Introduction. *Piers the Ploughman*, by William Langland, ed. J. F. Goodridge. Baltimore: Penguin, 1959.

Greg, W. W. "The Damnation of Faustus." *Modern Language Notes* 41 (1946): 97-107.

Griffiths, Paul. "The structure of prostitution in Elizabethan London." *Continuity and Change* 8 (1993): 39-63.

Haselkorn, Anne M. *Prostitution in Elizabethan and Jacobean Comedy*. Troy, N.Y.: Whitston, 1983.

Henderson, Joseph L., and Maud Oakes. *The Wisdom of the Serpent*. New York: George Braziller, 1963.

Henriques, Fernando. *Prostitution and Society*, 2 vols. London: MacGibbon & Kee, 1963.

Hoffman, Richard L. "Ovid and Chaucer's Myth of Theseus and Pirithous." *English Language Notes* 2 (1965): 252-57.

Huttar, Charles A. "Frail Grass and Firm Tree: David as a Model of Repentance in the Middle Ages and Early Renaissance." *The David Myth in Western Literature*, ed. Raymond-Jean Frontain and Jan Wojcik. West Lafayette, Ind.: Purdue University Press, 1980.

---. "Hell and The City: Tolkien and the Traditions of Western Literature." *A Tolkien Compass*, ed. Jared Lobdell. La Salle, Ill.: Open Court, 1975.

Johnson, David J. *Southwark and the City*. London: Oxford University Press, 1969.

Jones, H. S. V. *A Spenser Handbook*. New York: F. S. Crofts, 1930.

Jones, J. W. "Allegorical Interpretations in Servius." *Classical Journal* 56 (1961): 217-26.

Karras, Ruth Mazo. *Common Women: Prostitution and Sexuality in Medieval England*. New York: Oxford University Press, 1996.

---. "Sex, Money, and Prostitution in Medieval English Culture." In *Desire and Discipline: Sex and Sexuality in the Premodern West*, ed. Jacqueline Murray and Konrad Eisenbichler. Toronto: University of Toronto Press, 1996.

Kelly, Henry Ansgar. "Bishop, Prioress, and Bawd in the Stews of Southwark." *Speculum: A Journal of Medieval Studies* 75 (2000): 342-88.

Knight, W. F. Jackson. *Cumean gates*. Oxford: Blackwell, 1936.

---. *Roman Vergil*. London: Faber and Faber, 1944.

---. "Vergil and the Maze." *Classical Review* 43 (1929): 212-13.

---. *Vergil: Epic and Anthropology*. New York: Barnes & Noble, 1967.

Lenz, Joseph, "Base Trade: Theater as Prostitution." *ELH* 60 (1993): 833-56.

Lindley, K. J. "Riot Prevention and Control in Early Stuart London." *Transactions of the Royal Historical Society* 33 (1983): 109-26.

MacCulloch, J. A. *The Harrowing of Hell: A Comparative Study of an Early Christian Doctrine*. Edinburgh: T. & T. Clark, 1930.

Matthews, W. H. *Mazes and Labyrinths: Their History and Development*. New York: Dover, 1970.

McMullan, John L. *The Canting Crew: London's Criminal Underworld 1550-1700*. New Brunswick, N.J.: Rutgers University Press, 1984.

Milward, Peter. *Religious Controversies of the Elizabethan Age: A Survey of Primary Sources*. Lincoln: University of Nebraska Press, 1977.

Mullaney, Steven. *The Place of the Stage: License, Play, and Power in Renaissance England*. Chicago: University of Chicago Press, 1988.

Mulvey, Laura. *Visual and Other Pleasures*. London: Macmillan, 1989.

Myers, David G. *Social Psychology*, 7th ed. New York: McGraw-Hill, 2002.

New, John F. H. *Anglican and Puritan: The Basis of Their Opposition, 1558-1640*. Stanford, Calif.: Stanford University Press, 1964.

Norris, Margot. "Disenchanting Enchantment: The Theatrical Brothel of 'Circe.'" *Ulysses—En-Gendered Perspectives: Eighteen New Essays on the Episodes,* ed. Kimberly J. Devlin and Marilyn Reizbaum. Columbia, S.C.: University of South Carolina Press, 1999.

O'Connor, Sister Mary Catharine. *The Art of Dying Well: The Development of the Ars Moriendi*. New York: AMS, 1966.

Otis, Brooks. *Vergil: A Study in Civilized Poetry*. Oxford: Clarendon Press, 1963.

The Oxford English Dictionary, 2d ed. Oxford: Clarendon Press, 1989.

Patrides, C. A. "Renaissance and Modern Views on Hell." *Harvard Theological Review* 57 (1964): 217-36.

Pearson, D'Orsay W. "'Unkinde' Theseus: A Study in Renaissance Mythography." *English Literary Renaissance* 4 (1974): 276-98.

Pelling, Margaret. "Appearances and Reality: Barber Surgeons, the Body and Disease." In *London 1500-1700: The Making of the Metropolis*, ed. A. L. Beier and Roger Findlay. London: Longman, 1986.

Pfister, Manfred. *"The Passion* from Winterson to Coryate." *Venetian Views,*

Venetian Blinds: English Fantasies of Venice, ed. Manfred Pfister and Barbara Schaff. Amsterdam: Rodopi, 1999.

Putnam, C. J. *The Poetry of the Aeneid.* Cambridge, Mass.: Harvard University Press, 1963.

Rendle, William. "The Stews on Bankside." *Antiquarian Magazine & Bibliographer* 2 (1882): 70-77.

Salgādo, Gāmini. *The Elizabethan Underworld.* London: J. M. Dent, 1977.

Salisbury-Jones, G. T. *Street Life in Medieval England.* Totowa, N.J.: Rowman and Littlefield, 1975.

Scott, George Ryley. *Ladies of Vice: A History of Prostitution From Antiquity to the Present Day.* London: Tallis, 1968.

Seeman, Eric R. "'She Died Like Good Old Jacob': Deathbed Scenes and Inversions of Power in New England, 1675-1775." In *Proceedings of the American Antiquarian Society* 104 (1994): 285-314.

Seigel, Catharine F. "Hands Off The Hothouses: Shakespeare's Advice to the King." *Journal of Popular Culture* 20 (1986): 81-88.

Sharpe, J. A. *Crime in Early Modern England 1550-1750.* London: Longman, 1984.

Shugg, Wallace. "Prostitution in Shakespeare's London." *Shakespeare Studies* 10 (1977): 291-313.

Siena, Kevin P. "Pollution, Promiscuity, and the Pox: English Venereology and the Early Modern Medical Discourse on Social and Sexual Danger." *Journal of the History of Sexuality* 8 (1998): 553-74.

Snyder, Susan. "The Left Hand of God: Despair in Medieval and Renaissance Tradition." *Studies in the Renaissance* 12 (1965): 18-59.

Steadman, John M. "Milton and Patristic Tradition: The Quality of Hell Fire." *Anglia* 76 (1958): 116-28.

Still, Colin. *The Timeless Theme.* London: Ivor Nicholson & Watson, 1936.

Stone, Lawrence. *The Family, Sex and Marriage In England 1500-1800.* New

York: Harper & Row, 1977.

Strachan, Michael. *The Life and Adventures of Thomas Coryate.* London: Oxford University Press, 1962.

Walker, D. P. *The Decline of Hell: Seventeenth-Century Discussions of Eternal Torment.* Chicago: University of Chicago Press, 1964.

Wallace, Dewey D., Jr. "Puritan and Anglican: The Interpretation of Christ's Descent Into Hell and Elizabethan Theology." *Archive for Reformation History* 69 (1978): 248-87.

Webb, Henry J. "A Reinterpretation of Chaucer's Theseus." *Review of English Studies* 23 (1947): 289-96.

Winick, Charles, and Paul M. Kinsie. *The Lively Commerce: Prostitution in the United States.* Chicago: Quadrangle, 1971.

Zaleski, Carol. *Otherworld Journeys: Accounts of Near-Death Experience in Medieval and Modern Times.* New York: Oxford University Press, 1987.

Zarker, John W. "Aeneas and Theseus in *Aeneid* 6." *Classical Journal* 62 (1967): 220-26.

INDEX

STUDIES IN RENAISSANCE LITERATURE

1. J.M. Richardson, **Astrological Symbolism in Spenser's** *The Shepheardes Calender*: **The Cultural Background of a Literary Text**
2. Linda Kay Hoff, **Hamlet's Choice:** *Hamlet*-**A Reformation Allegory**
3. William Crelly, **Marcello Giovanetti (1598-1631) A Poet of the Early Roman Baroque**
4. Juan Luis Vives, *The Passions of the Soul*: **The Third Book of** *De Anima et Vita*, Carlos G. Noreña, (trans.)
5. Carlos G. Noreña, **A Vives Bibliography**
6. Robert F. Willson, Jr., **Shakespeare's Reflexive Endings**
7. Peter Milward, **The Mediaeval Dimension in Shakespeare's Plays**
8. Annwyl Williams, **Clement Marot: Figure, Text and Intertext**
9. Thomas O. Jones, **Renaissance Magic and Hermeticism in the Shakespeare Sonnets: Like Prayers Divine**
10. Carole Levin and Karen Robertson, (eds.), **Sexuality and Politics in Renaissance Drama**
11. W.R. Elton and E.A. Rauchut, co-compilers, **A Selective Annotated Bibliography of Shakespeare's** *Timon of Athens*
12. Louise Conley Jones, **A Textual Analysis of Marlowe's** *Doctor Faustus* **with Director's Book: Stage Action as Metaphor**
13. Dana F. Sutton (ed.), **The Complete Works of Thomas Watson, 1556-1592**; two volumes
14. John W. Crawford, **The Learning, Wit, and Wisdom of Shakespeare's Renaissance Women**
15. Anthony J. Gilbert, **Shakespeare's Dramatic Speech**
16. Joseph A. Ricapito, **Formalistic Aspects of Cervantes's** *Novelas ejemplares*
17. Gilian West, **A Dictionary of Shakespeare's Semantic Wordplay**
18. Farhang Zabeeh, **Shakespeare the Philosophical Poet**
19. Albert Rolls, **The Theory of the King's Two Bodies in the Age of Shakespeare**
20. Meera Tamaya, **An Interpretation of** *Hamlet* **Based on Recent Developments in Cognitive Studies**
21. Joanna Thompson, **The Character of Britomart in Spenser's** *The Faerie Queene*